Harry N. Abrams, Inc., Publishers

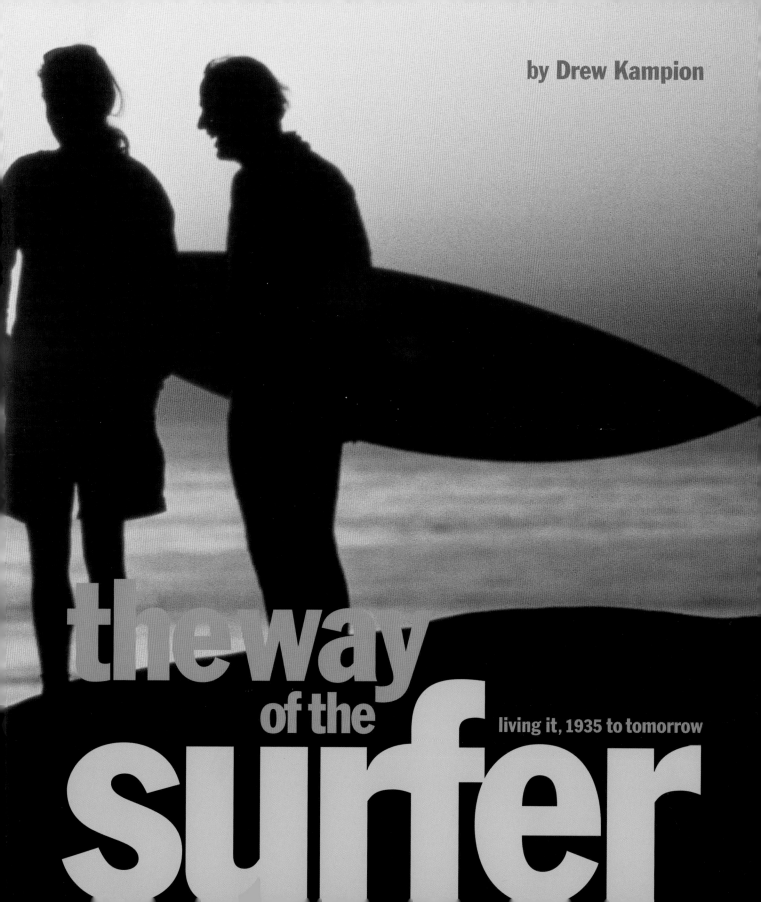

by Drew Kampion

the way
of the
surfer

living it, 1935 to tomorrow

For Susan

Editor: Richard Olsen
Designer: Russell Hassell
Production Manager: Stanley Redfern

Front cover: Looking toward the sun from beneath a
Fijian wave

Front endpages: The mother of all great surfing waves—
the spectacular Fijian vortex known as Teahupo'o

Back endpages: Surfer-crossing sign at "Swamis" in Encinitas,
California

Page 1: *Island Takeoff*, a fabric pattern created for Kahala
Sportswear by artist John Severson

Pages 2–3: End-of-session debriefing at Sunset Cliffs, California

Page 4: Swells approaching Sunset Beach, Oahu

LIBRARY OF CONGRESS CATALOGING-IN-PUBLICATION DATA

Kampion, Drew.
The way of the surfer / by Drew Kampion.—1st ed.
    p. cm.
ISBN 0-8109-4638-6 (hardcover : alk. paper)
1. Surfing. 2. Surfers. I. Title.
GV840.S8.K37 2003
797.3'2—dc21

2003004500

Text copyright © 2003 Drew Kampion

Published in 2003 by Harry N. Abrams, Incorporated, New York

Printed and bound in China
10 9 8 7 6 5 4 3 2 1

 Harry N. Abrams, Inc.
100 Fifth Avenue
New York, NY 10011
www.abramsbooks.com

Abrams is a subsidiary of
LA MARTINIÈRE
GROUPE

Contents

The teacher in the classroom: Kelly Slater
in the barrel at Hollow Trees, Indonesia,
during the 1999 "Tomorrowland" *surfari*,
chronicled in Jack Johnson's 2002 film
The September Sessions.

Introduction

Surfing is the simple act of walking on water. There are many other ways to ride ocean waves (bodysurfing, for example), but when we say "surfing," we really mean walking on water, or at least standing on it. This is what makes surfing unique—when we surf, we walk on water. But this "simple" act is so complex, it's hard to believe it's possible at all. Consider the progression of forces that birth ocean waves—the action of solar radiation on the upper atmosphere, the migration of that energy toward the surface, how it joins with the planet's rotational and counter-rotational currents to create jet-stream flows and, finally, surface winds. Consider the movement of wind over water, the steady friction of air on the liquid surface, ruffling it into ripples, nudging up chop, pushing up seas, and the resulting turbulent fields of wind-tossed seas that become well-formed bands of open-ocean swell.

Propelled by gravity, trains of swell race away from the winds that spawned them, moving across the ocean deeps until they feel the drag of the shallows near land. As the swells shoal, they rise up out of themselves, peaking and curling into the liquid dreams that surfers ride. And if the generation of waves is complex, consider the intricate physics of the controlled fall of riding them. It would take more than a few chalkboards to plot the calculations.

Reducing all this to simple phrases, one could say that surfing is nearly incomprehensible, almost miraculous, exquisitely sensual, and perhaps unique to this one blue planet.

Surfing is often described as an ancient Hawaiian sport; it was, and it still is. The "experts" reckon it all started in Polynesia before the year 1000, but no one really knows. The cultures of the Pacific islands were expressed in stone and bone, not iron and parchment, and little has been preserved from that era. Nonetheless, around the time of the Vikings does make sense, since there seems to be a resonance in human affairs expressed in a synchronicity of events. It was during the eighth, ninth, and tenth centuries that these Scandinavian warriors were raiding Europe with fierce abandon. They are still regarded as the best sailors of their age by historians who fail to take into account the contemporaneous exploits of the Polynesians.

Those natives of the South Pacific built large voyaging canoes out of forest hardwood and stabilized the big hulls with outriggers. These vessels could sail closer to weather than any European monohull, and (like the Vikings' long ships) when the winds were light or straight on the nose, they could be paddled. Powered by sails of woven pandanus leaves and the athletes who manned her, the voyaging canoe was a notable achievement in maritime architecture. Guided by peerless navigators, ancient Polynesians were accustomed to long journeys at sea, either as part of their traditional trading routes or as adventurous explorations. Out on the immense blue desert of the Pacific they discovered Rapa Nui (Easter Island), the Hawaiian chain, and hundreds of other remote islands.

The Polynesians were true voyagers. They knew the sea much as the Sioux peoples knew the North American prairies. They could "see" islands hundreds of miles away in the refractory patterns on the liquid plain they rode. They were masters of celestial navigation. They routinely made crossings of over a thousand miles and hit their target islands dead on. They were very tuned into the environment, and their far-flung trade circles operated on a seasonal calendar with a punctuality that presaged the celebrated German rail system.

How exactly they discovered surfing will never be known for sure, but you can conjecture. Any sailor, paddler, or rower knows the dynamics of the ocean

surface—the cycles of energy, the patterns of the sea, how everything comes in waves—the seasons, the storms, the tides, and the surf. Out on the ocean, paddling with the swells, you can feel the presence of the next wave coming up behind you—how it draws you back on its approach, then lifts you—quite a bit if the swell is large—and propels you ahead as the face of it passes under you. And sometimes if you're moving fast enough and the wave is steep enough, you start chasing down its forward slope, the hull slapping rudely on the chop as you lift your paddle over your head and let the wave take you for a ride.

Perhaps surfing started something like that, catching a free ride on the way back in from fishing, resting the paddle and enjoying the glide. The logical next step was to play the sport—to stand up and show off. However, when the great eighteenth-century European explorers (notably Captain James Cook and his fleet) came upon Polynesia and first saw people riding waves, they were confused. Early renderings reveal their misapprehensions—naked maidens balancing gracefully on small planks atop aquatic billows—positions that defy now-understood hydrodynamic principles.

The arrival of British sailors and Christian missionaries unleashed a double-edged Hawaiian genocide (to a large degree unintended), a little Pacific holocaust of disease and cultural disruption. The survivors worked in the new plantation economy, and surfing fell by the wayside. Mostly.

In 1874, savvy traveler Isabella L. Bird spent a day at a remote beach and observed more accurately, "The great art seems to be to mount the roller precisely at the right time, and to keep exactly on its curl just before it breaks . . . always apparently coming down hill with a slanting motion . . . always just ahead of the breaker, carried shoreward by its mighty impulse at the rate of forty miles an hour . . . the more daring riders knelt and even stood on their surf-boards, waving their arms and uttering exultant cries . . . always apparently on the verge of engulfment by the fierce breaker whose towering white crest was ever above and just behind them" (Isabella L. Bird, *The Hawaiian Archipelago: Six Months Among the Palm Groves, Coral Reefs, and Volcanoes of the Sandwich Islands,* John Murray: London, 1876).

That was just the afterglow of Polynesian surfing, a moment discovered in a rare, persisting enclave of the past. Nobody really knows exactly what surfing was like in its full glory. It is clear that at the time of European contact in 1778 (forgetting for a moment any shipwrecked Spaniards who may or may not have washed ashore on Niihau 200 years earlier), surfing was a highly regarded and integral part of Hawaiian culture. Kings and queens did it. Princes and princesses did it. Kahunas and warriors did it. And so did most everyone else.

They surfed the waves on a variety of vehicles. They rode short, wide, thin *paipo* boards on their bellies; they rode the longer and thicker *alai'a* boards prone,

kneeling, or erect, but the royal eighteen-foot-long, cigar-shaped *olo* was only ridden by very important people at exclusive surf spots.

One of these special areas was far off the beach at Waikiki, out by Diamond Head, a spot the old Hawaiians called Kalahuewehe. Many a great surfing contest was held there during the annual convergence of the Hawaiian peoples on this island they called "the gathering place." And what the Polynesians liked about the place, the *haoles* (white foreigners) did, too.

Following the 1893 hostile overthrow of Queen Liliuokalani by resident Americans, missionary son Sanford B. Dole became president of the short-lived Republic of Hawaii in 1894. The Spanish-American War immediately swept the obscure Pacific island chain into national consciousness. When someone grasped the strategic significance of Pearl Harbor to the nation's security, the game was over. Hawaii was annexed to the United States in 1898 and became a U.S. territory in 1900 with Dole installed as governor. Honolulu was the territorial capital, Waikiki was the beach, and the good old days began.

"Half a mile out, where is the reef, the whiteheaded combers thrust suddenly skyward out of the placid turquoise-blue and come rolling into shore. One after another they come, a mile long, with smoking crests, the white battalions of the infinite army of the sea. . . . And suddenly, out there where a big smoker lifts skyward, rising like a sea-god from out of the welter of spume and churning white, on the giddy, toppling, overhanging and down-falling, precarious crest appears the dark head of a man. Swiftly he rises through the rushing white. His black shoulders, his chest, his loins, his limbs—all is abruptly projected on one's vision. Where but the moment before was only the wide desolation and invincible roar, is now a man, erect, full-statured, not struggling frantically in that wild movement, not buried and crushed and buffeted by those mighty monsters, but standing above them all, calm and superb, poised on the giddy summit, his feet buried in the churning foam, the salt smoke rising to his knees, and all the rest of him in the free air and flashing sunlight, and he is flying through the air, flying forward, flying fast as the surge on which he stands. He is a Mercury—a brown Mercury. . . . He is a Kanaka—and more, he is a man, a member of the kingly species that has mastered matter and the brutes and lorded it over creation" (Jack London, "A Royal Sport: Surfing at Waikiki" from *The Cruise of the Snark*).

When "walking on water" caught the eye of adventure author Jack London in 1907, most of the native population of Hawaii was dead and gone, and missionaries and plantation economics had reshaped the island paradise. There were only a handful of Hawaiian surfers left, and most congregated on the beach at Waikiki, where the *kanuks* could make a living introducing the arcane practice to *haole*

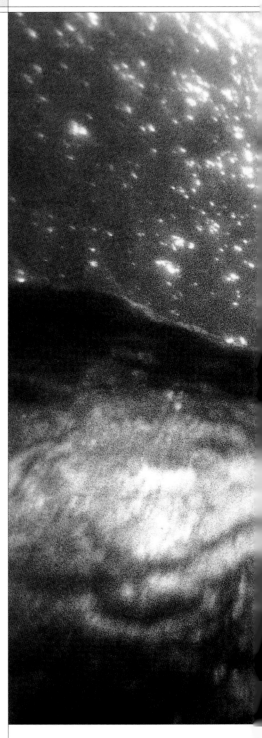

tourists, whose interest in the sport was sparked by the writings of London, Mark Twain, and others. A select group of experts worked as "beachboys," taking visitors on tandem rides and giving surfing lessons. Between customers they hung out on the sand, played the ukulele, sang, talked story, made love to *haole* women, surfed, paddled canoe, and generally had a pretty easygoing lifestyle. They were the grandfathers of modern surfing.

This core group of Waikiki surfers seeded the twentieth-century renaissance of "the sport of Hawaiian kings." With their knowledge of the ocean, their fearless play in the powerful waves, and most of all their confident, self-sufficient style, they inspired those who came to Waikiki. A few notable beachboys traveled to other parts of the world, taking surfing with them, and seeding its growth else-where. Through this small band of beachboys, surfing passed forward into our modern era, where it has assumed an increasingly important place in global culture.

Vilified as a beatnik tribe of beach bums in the late 1950s and early '60s, the postmodern view of surfers has shifted, informed by the growing complexity of the sport itself in recent decades. Bold new gymnastic approaches to wave riding have combined with the proliferation of lifestyle-related "board sports" to capture increasing media attention (surfing has gone mainstream). At the same time, technology, in the guise of personal watercraft (jet skis or PWCs), have opened access to the "unridden realm"—giant waves that generally break farther out to sea and cannot be approached without "jet-assisted take-off" methodologies, by which the surfer is towed into a wave that he couldn't physically generate enough speed to paddle into. The sight of diminu-tive surfers dwarfed by sixty-foot walls of raging water has been compelling enough to put surfing, at last, on par with the other so-called "extreme" sports that occupy so much of our precious attention in this current neo-Roman epoch.

But beneath this highly visible world of danger, disaster, and fleeting glory, there lives and breathes the "rank and file" surf culture—a million or more so-called hardcore devotees, each with a personal relationship with the ocean and its waves. To represent surfing as the achievements of only its greatest practitioners on the most epic of waves is a misleading shorthand—a symbolic gesture in the direction of the infinite truths residing deep in the oceanic reservoirs of our combined surfing experiences. It sounds pretentious, but it's not meant to be. It's just simple math.

The history of surfing is the sum total of all the waves ever ridden, of all the journeys and adventures and lessons learned by all those who have ever paddled out to ride a wave—an impossible story to tell, of course, even as reflected in the lives of a few tribal archetypes, individuals who embody the essence of the endeavor, whose lives along the surfer's path are tantamount to walking on water.

USA 37

DUKE KAHANAMOKU

2002

**D**uke Kahanamoku (1880–1968) and his brothers were among the original Waikiki beachboys. A pure Hawaiian, Kahanamoku was a great all-around waterman and a swimming sensation, winning Olympic gold medals in 1912 (Antwerp) and 1920 (Stockholm). On a return trip across America, he introduced surfing to the East Coast. In 1914, Kahanamoku was invited to Australia, where, after breaking his own world record for the 100-yard freestyle (53.8 seconds), he demonstrated the ancient Hawaiian sport at Freshwater Beach near Sydney, to great acclaim.

Irish-Hawaiian George Freeth (1883–1919) was a Waikiki beachboy, regarded by contemporaries as the best surfer of the era. He was brought to California in 1907 by developer Henry E. Huntington to demonstrate the sport of Hawaiian kings to astonished throngs at Redondo Beach, terminus of Huntington's new rail line. Freeth stayed on to become the prototypical modern lifeguard, establishing the sort of professional standards that have made California the world model in beach safety.

Tom Blake (1902–1994) was a larger-than-life surf pioneer, a seminal force in the history of the sport, who came out of the north woods of Wisconsin to almost single-handedly transform surfing from a primitive Polynesian curiosity into a twentieth-century lifestyle. Blake built a waterproof housing for his 4 × 5 camera so he could take close-up pictures of surfers at Waikiki in the late 1920s; he wrote the first book on surfing, *Hawaiian Surfboard* (1935), in which he discussed surfing's mythological and historical roots as well as its technique.

Ancient "pre-Contact" Hawaiian surfboards had been made from breadfruit, wiliwili, and koa woods, but redwood was the material of choice in the early 1900s. The clear-grain old-growth timber was resistant to water damage and relatively light. Still, a nine-foot-long, two-foot-wide surfboard might weigh eighty or 100 pounds, and Waikiki beachboys used bigger and heavier redwood boards to take their customers on tandem rides. By necessity, surfing was almost exclusively a man's sport.

Inspired by the ancient surfboards he discovered at Honolulu's Bishop Museum (Hawaii's museum of national and cultural history since 1889), Blake created streamlined, lightweight boards for surfing and paddleboarding that brought the early-1900s surfing renaissance to a crescendo, before World War II. While some surfers continued to ride the redwood "planks," many rode Blake's hollow "cigar boxes." Still others were inspired to innovate, and the evolution of the modern surfboard (and the performance revolution that accompanied it) commenced.

By the 1930s, surfing had tenuous footholds in several parts of the world. Thriving subcultures had developed at some strategic beaches, most notably San Onofre, at the northern boundary of San Diego County. There, stimulated by firsthand accounts from steamship stowaways to the mecca of Waikiki, a surfing-based community blossomed in the pre–World War II era. Satellited by like-minded enthusiasts at Windansea Beach (San Diego) and Malibu (Los Angeles), and referenced by smaller enclaves in Santa Cruz, California, and in Texas and Florida, surfing enjoyed a new age of discovery.

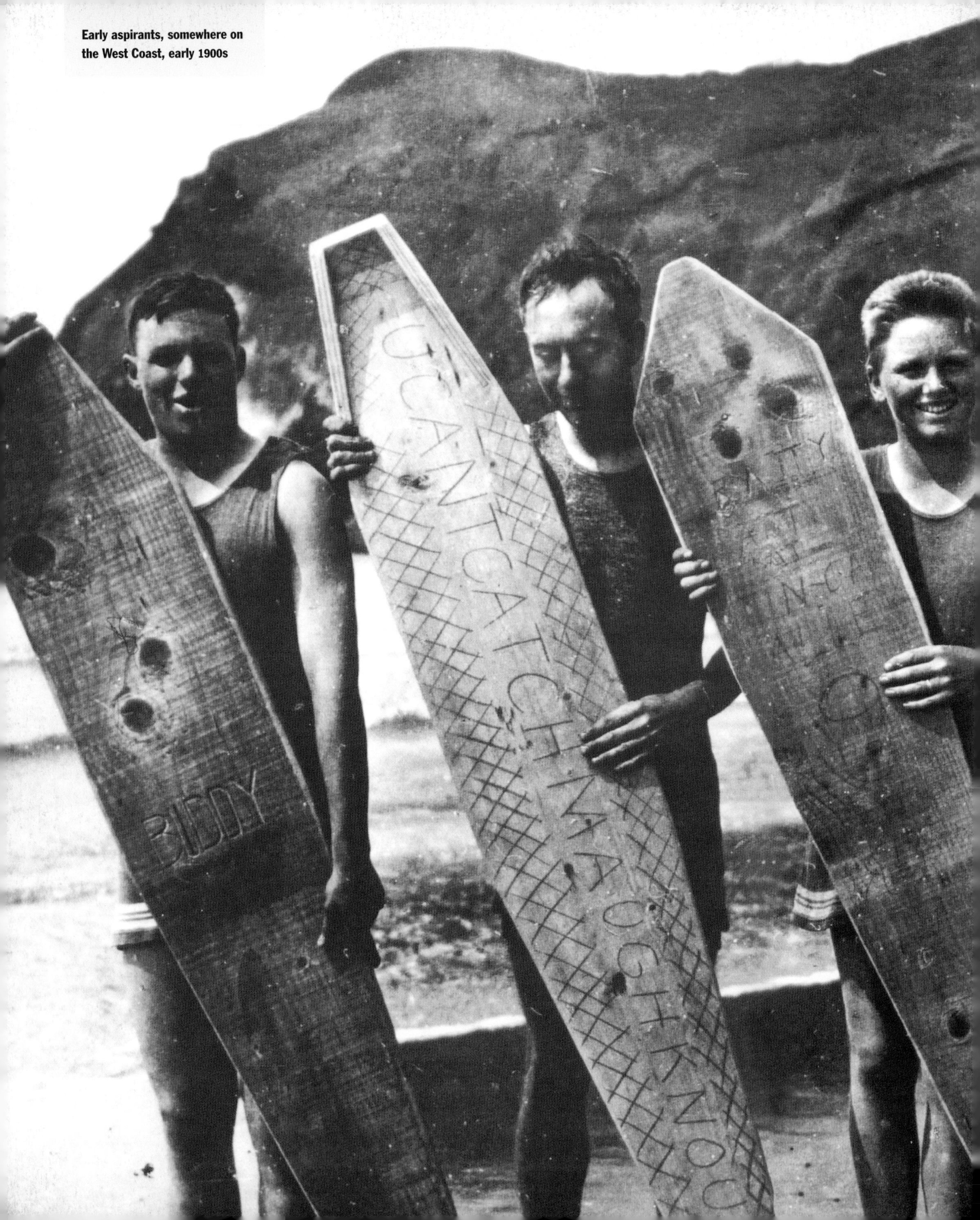

Early aspirants, somewhere on the West Coast, early 1900s

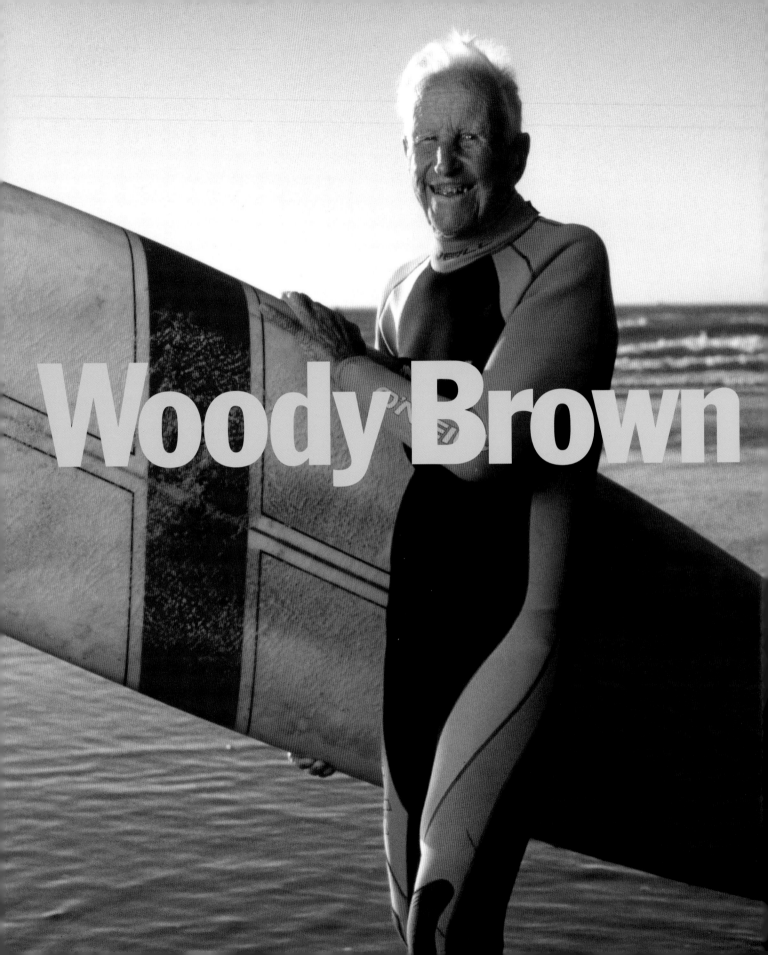

Woody Brown

Soaring

THE SPIRITUAL JOURNEY OF WOODY BROWN

Woody Brown in
California, 2000

The road into Kahului—the Hana Highway turning into Ka'ahumanu Avenue—used to be pretty low-key, parts of it downright rural. Now it's a divided four-lane affair with turning lanes and signals at every corner, large malls left and right. Even the surf and windsurf shops look like malls. It's easy to get lost and forget where you are, which is on Maui, one of a cluster of mountaintops that have erupted in the middle of the Pacific Ocean. ❧ Across the road from Kahului Harbor is the Harbor Lights condominium complex, a lone, large building surrounded by heavily regulated parking lots. A block long and stacked high, its half-dozen rows of identical windows face out on the harbor. Woody Brown's is three stories up, about twenty across.

One afternoon in January of 2001, we stand at his window looking out on the harbor. Although the opening in the jetties is scarcely a short city-block long, big winter swells can squeeze through and fan in toward the beach, peaking and spilling over on several reefs, producing fun small-wave surf. It is flat now, but Woody points out the spots anyway. The peak to the west is his favorite.

I'd seen his wife Macrene briefly when I'd come in—young, jet-haired, bright-eyed—but she has taken Woody Jr. (a handsome fifteen-year-old) off to town, so that Woody and I could sit on the big leatherette sofa and talk. Woody wears his short-sleeved shirt, mostly unbuttoned, and a pair of beach shorts. His rubber thongs are parked by the doorway. His old Ole surfboard leans against the wall under the big window. Another one—the blue Angulo—is propped under the bedroom window. Otherwise, I see few visible artifacts of his surfing life. This is partially explained by a small tragedy: a box filled with precious cargo—his old photographs and memorabilia—was lost some years ago when he moved here.

It occurs to me that the lean old man sitting next to me—with sun-weathered skin, piercing blue eyes, the shock of white hair, and a near-perpetual and almost toothless smile—is very likely what some would call a transcendent being. Since I'm not exactly an expert in transcendent beings (although I've been in the company of a few people who claimed to be such blessed individuals), I can't be sure. But who more likely? The arc of this man's life—his path— seems to have dragged him, kicking and screaming, straight into the arms of revelation. Two falls from the sky, a dozen or so brushes with death here or there, encounters with the paranormal and/or astral planes, the powerful loss of a soul mate, miraculous survivals against great odds, and finally, as a forty-year-old agnostic, Woody experienced contact. When he tells me about it, it's like hearing the other shoe drop. It all makes sense.

Woody wearing a grin and a lei. Waikiki Beach, 1946

WOODBRIDGE PARKER BROWN WAS BORN in New York City on January 5, 1912. His family was blue blood, listed on the New York 400, but Woody was less impressed with high society than with the young fliers out at Curtis Field on Long Island. There, he met aviator Charles Lindbergh in the months before the Lone Eagle's historic trans-Atlantic solo flight of 1927. Woody learned to fly a Curtiss JN-4, "Jenny," an obsolete single-engine trainer used by the U.S. Army Air Service in World War I. After a while, he transitioned to gliders, preferring silence and the rush of wind to the racket of the barnstorming machine. He soon met an elegant Englishwoman with an adventurous spirit that loved (but did not match) his own, and away they went out West to San Diego in '35.

The young couple lived at La Jolla, where Woody discovered waves. He started out bodysurfing, then, in a stroke of primal intuition, he got stuck on the idea of building a vehicle to ride them. "I didn't know if anyone else surfed in the world! I just built this plywood box, y'know?" The hollow plywood box soon gave way to a more streamlined shape in which he adapted some of the aerodynamic wisdom he'd acquired to the denser medium of water. He called this surfboard the Snowshoe. His friend Towny Cromwell saw it and had to have one too, so Woody helped him build it.

"We just laid down riding," Woody recalls with obvious amazement. "It never occurred to us to stand up, until one day Towny says, 'Hey! You know, in Hawaii they stand up!' And I says, 'Well, what do they do *that* for?' And he says, 'I don't know.' But, so . . . we started standing up, too!" He laughs a big laugh. "Life is amazing, isn't it? He worked for Scripps [the Scripps Institute of Oceanography] in La Jolla; they named the Cromwell Current after him. A humble, nice boy—not arrogant. He was killed in a plane crash in Mexico—so sad."

Big surf at Makaha Beach on Oahu, 1953, with Bob Simmons on the left, Flippy Hoffman squatting, and Woody angling below

Betty and Woody both had small incomes from their respective fathers, "so between the two we were doin' all right. We weren't millionaires, but if we were careful we could rent a house and have food and . . . you know what I mean. In other words, we were the richest people in the *world!* Right? Not too much, but a little bit—that's the deal."

In pioneering glider flights off the cliffs of nearby Torrey Pines, Woody survived a couple of near-death experiences to become a soaring champion, winning meets around the state and country. In the midst of "the happiest years of my life," his wife died in childbirth and Woody "cracked up" in earnest. He gave up the baby to relatives and headed out to lose himself in the South Pacific. He got as far as Hawaii. War was imminent, and passports and visas weren't being issued. They wouldn't let him leave.

Trapped, out of his mind with loss, he aimlessly wandered the islands—on foot or on an old bicycle—a skinny, spaced-out *haole* with nowhere to call home. The Hawaiians welcomed him in with warmth and Aloha. Before long, he met Rachel, a local hotel entertainer, whose boyfriend had recently died. They hit it off, married, and moved into a small apartment on the beach above the Waikiki Tavern. While "Ma" Brown stayed home with the babies, Woody, a conscientious objector, performed his national service as a government surveyor, a job that took him to Christmas Island, now part of Kiribati, where he got his first ride on an outrigger canoe, a craft so swift and responsive that it inspired him to research, design, and build the first modern catamaran based on traditional Polynesian multihulls.

Throughout those years, Woody continued to surf, gradually ratcheting up to the big waves. Woody talks about surfing in Hawaii in the early 1940s: "When I came to Hawaii, there was a clique of boys that used to go out in big waves. There was only about four or five of 'em that would go out there in these tremendous twenty- and twenty-five-foot waves. None of the beach-boys would go out there, but I had been riding big waves in La Jolla—we'd gotten up to about fifteen feet—so I just automatically joined with these boys, and they took me in." Woody joined them and became a fixture at Makaha, on the island's west side, and on pioneering expeditions to the now-famous North Shore, which encompasses the legendary surf spots Waimea Bay, Banzai Pipeline, and Sunset Beach. They nicknamed him Spider because, "I surf with my arms all out, and I'm half squatting down, and I'm skinny with my long legs,

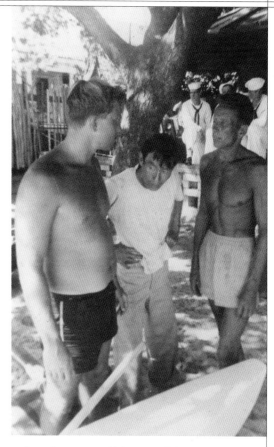

and I guess I look like a big spider riding the board."

That so-called "clique"— John Kelly, Fran Heath, George Downing, Rus Takaki, Wally Froiseth, and Rabbit Kekai—was the Hot Curl crew, so named for their small, streamlined surfboards, which stuck tenaciously to the hollow curl of a wave. Woody describes how Kelly first whittled down his "slide-ass" swastika-style surfboard to a three-inch vee-tail. That was in '37.

"They had evolved that board, and of course I shaped my boards like that, with them there. The only difference was, I could build faster boards to get across those big waves because of my glider-flying experience. In other words, I understood how air flowed around things, and then I read how water is incompressible, so therefore it would have to follow the curve, whereas in an airplane, if the curve gets too steep, the air just breaks away in turbulence if it can't follow the curve. But in water, because it's incompressible, the water has to follow the curve, and that's why, when he [Kelly] rounded the backend [of his surfboard], it couldn't go down sideways, because the water couldn't go around that curved stern that fast. So I understood all that from my flying—that any kind of curve in the water is gonna slow the board down because the water has a hard time getting around that curve—and I could make my boards much faster, and I could get across these great big waves when nobody else could."

These new vehicles seemed designed for the challenging surf off Oahu's North Shore. It was there, three days before Christmas of '43, that Woody's most notorious surf session occurred. He and a young man named Dickie Cross paddled out at Sunset Beach on a rising swell. They were caught outside and couldn't make it back to the beach; they eventually paddled four miles down the coast to Waimea, where they figured they had a chance of making it to the beach through the deepwater bay. Woody survived, while Cross never was found.

Opposite: Inspired by native craft he saw in Samoa during World War II, Woody incorporated the concept of asymmetric hulls with his prototype catamaran. Waikiki Beach, 1946

Woody and Albert Kumalae talking catamaran theory with an interested tourist at Waikiki

Woody laughs softly, remembering that evening. The waves were giant. They'd paddled all the way to Waimea, and now Cross was way inside toward the beach and had lost his board off the rocky point. Woody decided to go in after him, but just then, an outside set blackened the horizon. The last sight he had of Cross was the look of wide-eyed surprise and dread on the man's face, seeing his approaching doom. Then Woody pushed his own board away and dove for the bottom. It was dark when he finally crawled ashore at Waimea Bay.

The cloud of that event—the killer-wave reputation of the North Shore—remained intact for some fourteen years until Waimea was finally "conquered" in November of '57. By then, the Browns had moved to Maui, where Woody supported Rachel and their two children by farming.

THE AREA CALLED KULA IS ON THE WEST SLOPE of Haleakalā. At the 4,000-foot level, where Woody and Rachel bought a small farm, there is a commanding view of the narrow neck of Maui, from Kahului on the north shore to Maʻalaea on the south. Back in the early '50s, Woody had Maui's best waves almost all to himself.

"When I came here, there was one surfing place—Hoʻokipa, and the city had built lockers for the boys there, and they rode just way up in the corner where the waves don't get too big, by the pavilion. But I liked to ride big waves, and I had a board that could ride the big waves."

The locals had hollow Tom Blake–style boards or the old slide-ass planks, "so they never rode big waves; their deal was seven or eight feet, *pau*, that was the end. But I liked the ten-, fifteen-, twenty-foot waves. But this one boy, Donald Chimura, he was kind of interested in my board, and so I helped him build one like it, and we went all around the island here finding new places— Honolua and Maʻalaea [on Maui's West Shore] and all over—and he and I were the only ones that would go out in these big waves."

Woody was truck farming to pay the bills, working the land, growing vegetables —cabbage, carrots, string beans, tomatoes—driving them to market, making forty bucks a month, sometimes more, and going surfing when the swell was up. And then he tells me the story:

"I was still riding big waves, so one day I was out there in my yard working on my surfboard," he begins. "Now, you won't believe all this, boy!" He laughs, then continues. "So, I'm workin' up there—quiet. There wasn't another house for a mile around; you could hear a pin drop. So, I'm workin' the surfboard, and all of a sudden, this voice says, 'What're you doin'?' And it kind of startled me because there was nobody around, but I just say, 'Whoa . . . I'm just workin' on my surfboard.' I mean, it was said in such a nice way, just like some guy standing there who really wanted to know. So . . . a couple of minutes more, then it said, 'What for?' And I said, 'Well, I'm making it faster, so I can get across these great big waves.' And then it blew my mind, see? Because then it said, 'But you can't take it with you when you go.' Who-who-whooooo!" Suddenly, Woody is laughing with the shock and thrill, remembering.

"That just *blew* my mind out! Because I don't believe in God—I believe in this world—here!—and the flying and the surfing. But now he's blown my mind, and I said, 'Well, what *can* you take with you when you go?' And the awful answer was, 'Nothing!'" And then Woody is laughing again, echoing his original amazement. "That blew my mind totally. So I said, 'Well, then this world is a damn lie and a deception! It has no real meaning at all! What good is it if you can't take anything with you?' And so I was blown out, you see? I *saw* you can't take it with you when you go."

Woody says his life changed from that moment on. Suddenly he had no faith in anything. He thought he was going to die, literally. But then, "Wait a minute!" he realized, "I can't die; I've got a beautiful wife and two children. It's my fault! I created them!" He searched his mind, considering the great men of history—Buddha, Jesus, Confucius, even Einstein—and finally came to rest on Jesus, who died to save us, said "turn the other cheek," and "love and forgive your enemy." He was led, he tells me, to understand that Satan was the power of our "separate" thought, which keeps us from understanding God, who sees everything in wholeness. What Woody came to know, understand, and finally experience fully is that, "God is love."

"That's what Jesus told them on the Mount," Woody explained, "love and forgive your neighbor. But nobody will do it! The Church doesn't do it. Nobody will do it. But I *did it*, you see? Maybe I'm a fruit, but that's beside the point. *I did it*."

Being so obviously God-intoxicated, I wonder how important surfing could be to him. "Is surfing wasting your life on the earth?" I ask.

"No, no, no!" he proclaims. "Surfing exercises your whole body, and you're exposing yourself to nature. See, if you go in a gymnasium and do this [calisthenics], you're exercising this, but the rest of your body isn't doin' much of anything.

Woody tucking into a long wall, a massive wave for the day and its equipment, at Makaha, c. 1950

But as soon as you expose yourself to nature, then the nature within you is sort of fighting back! Surfing is good because it gets all the boys away from the street corners telling dirty stories! Y'know what I mean? It gets 'em all with nature! And it's a clean, healthy sport that builds your body, so I think it's a very fine thing. It saved *my* life a couple times."

Woody believes that life on earth is a kind of laboratory for spiritual development. "I believe the whole human being is in the process of evolution," he says. "I've come to understand that everything is in the process of growth—whether it's a tree or a human being. But it's not an evolution that takes thousands of years; it's condensed to a very short period, which is what we call growth. Evolution and growth are the same thing. God isn't stagnant and dead—he grows, he's evolving, too. Everything is growing; the law of life is growth! Simple as that. There's no life without growth; nothing is stagnant."

"So God has to grow. If he was just satisfied with everything he had, that would get boring, wouldn't it? I mean, that's why the rich man is so damn unhappy, because he's got everything—he's bored to death. So a principle is that God has to grow too, and we are the new growth of God! We are the new child of God, and we've come to be with Him, and we're added to Him, and He becomes greater because of us. Isn't that a beautiful, wonderful story?"

Left: Small waves are often tougher to ride than big ones. Woody at age 89, surfing Launiupoko on Maui

Right: Woody finds his path through the reef at Launiupoko

God–intoxicated Woody in front of his condominium in Kahului, Maui, 2001

But the world doesn't look so wonderful at times, I remind him. He agrees. "We're crazy, aren't we? We're just crazy! I mean, the mind is sick. The whole human race is sick! But there's a reason for it, so it's all right, see? Once you understand that, that it couldn't be any other way, that's the only way we're gonna learn to have understanding. It's through this fighting and bickering, and that creates the ability to understand, which is necessary in order to keep the spirit world going, so it's all right, see?"

Woody has written a book, *The Gospel of Love: A Revelation of the Second Coming*. "It's a spiritual translation of the Bible," he tells me. "Can you imagine— ME!? When the Lord came to me, he said, 'You're gonna write a book.' And I said, 'Oh? Well . . . okay. And then he said, 'It's gonna be a spiritual translation of the Bible,' and I went, 'Awwwww [wailing] . . . but I don't KNOW anything about the Bible!' And the Lord said, 'Nevermind, I'll tell you what to write.' Since publishing *The Gospel of Love* in '80, Woody has been working on a second volume. Woody was featured in David L. Brown's award-winning '99 documentary, *Surfing for Life;* some would say he stole the show.

ONE SUMMER MANY YEARS AGO, when the surf was flat on the north side, Woody found a good little surf spot out by Maui's Lahaina, near a place called Laniupoko. "I guess I didn't want to fight the whitewater all the time, so I found this place that had a deep hole inside, so when you lost your board, it didn't go up on the rocks. And not only that, but there was a little channel between the surf to go out, where it didn't break unless it was tremendous. So, that was neat; I loved that. They called it Woody Surf because I was the only one that'd go out there." He cleared a path from the beach through the sharp rocks to the waves and made it a ritual to clear that cleft of white sand when he returned each summer.

On this January day, I watch Woody secure his leash around his waist and walk his board through this path. Then he smoothly hops into a knee-paddling position and strokes out to the peak, where he rides wave after wave, looking fluid, controlled, and thoroughly at home.

Woody has lived the picaresque life of a Parsifal—the Holy Fool of Arthurian legend, who blundered innocently, nonetheless heroically, into selfless risk after selfless risk. Or maybe in Woody's case it wasn't always so selfless; maybe his pursuit of freedom, adventure, and discovery was initially based solidly in the realm of the senses and the ego, but it's certain that the man's fate was carrying him along in spite of—not because of—some sense of self. He's gone way beyond that now. If you were looking for a word to describe this ninety-year-old surfer today, "saint" would come to mind.

"I think death is a great and wonderful thing to look forward to," Woody tells me, and I remind him of what Bob Dylan wrote: "Just remember that death is not the end."

"Bob Simmons made this surfboard for fifteen-year-old Tom Carlin in 1950. Carlin became a lifeguard, a Navy Seal, and an underwater movie extra. The board is a veteran of big surf in the Tijuana Sloughs and at Windansea and on the North Shore. I took this picture with a great old Nikon camera. It has a message for me and represents the death of Simmons. All that remains is his legend in stories and his application of hydrodynamic principals in creating the modern surfboard. With Simmons, a new profile came into being. If you look closely, you can still see it in today's surfboards."—John Elwell

World War II pulled most surfers off the beach, some of them never to return. But a permanent arm injury kept California Institute of Technology engineering student Bob Simmons home in California with those too young or otherwise unfit to go. He quit school and went to work as a mathematician for Douglas Aircraft, but his newfound passion was surfing. His mother helped him load his seventy-five-pound board onto his car, and he had to drag it down the beach to get to the surf. He worked nights or abandoned his job when the waves were good. He was good at what he did, so they took him back after the swells died down.

Simmons (1919–1954) was an eccentric young genius who lived a spartan existence (soy beans!) and liked his solitude. On the day the atomic bomb was dropped on Hiroshima (August 6, 1945) there was great surf at Malibu, and Simmons ranted all day in the lineup. "They'll ruin the world with this bomb!" he screamed in disgust. By the end of the war, he had applied his considerable technical skills to surfboard design.

Simmons and post–World War II apprentices Matt Kivlin (b. 1929) and Joe Quigg (b. 1925) integrated new materials like Styrofoam, fiberglass, and plastic resin systems into their surfboard designs. Most of their experimentation took place at Malibu. Quigg translated Simmons's hydro- and aero-dynamic concepts into more streamlined surfboards that drew on Blake's paddleboard templates as well as the foiled shape of the Hawaiian "hot curl" boards of the period. Sheathing his balsa-wood shapes in fiberglass and polyester resin yielded the strong, lightweight boards nicknamed "potato chips." The addition of a fin, or skeg, in the early '50s created the heightened maneuverability, which Kivlin exploited on Malibu's long, smooth waves, introducing a casual style of surfing that echoed the insouciant poses and mannerisms demonstrated by aficionados of the newly emerging biker gangs of inland California.

The hot war was gone, but the Cold War remained. From the perspective of riding waves, it all was irrelevant. Somewhere between the Beat Generation and Hollywood, there was the beach, and the obscure sport of surfing was quietly thriving. The scene at Malibu was emblematic—a bohemian sideshow to the good life of the inland valleys and their concomitant American values. Fifteen-year-old Kathy Kohner spent the summer of '56 under the charismatic tutelage of various *kahunas,* party animals, and surf rats. In the fall, her father Fred used her experiences to write the story that bore her surfer nickname—*Gidget* (for girl midget). The book was a surprising success, and the 1959 movie version ended surfing's relatively obscure incubation period. Books, movies, magazines, and surf music followed. Simultaneous innovations in polyurethane-foam technology made the virtual mass-production of surfboards a reality as throngs of inspired inlanders flocked to the coast. Surfing was hot, and the masters of southern California wave riding became cult heroes. The big three:

M ICKEY D ORA (1934–2002), stepson of pioneer stylist Gard Chapin and an admirer of Kivlin's approach to wave riding, defined surfing's enduring rejection of authority, riding waves with nonchalant grace, "tapping" the occasional "kook" who got in his way, and eloquently sharing his disgust over the growth and exploitation of surfing with the sport's budding media. He left California in the '70s to live most of the rest of his life in a wandering exile.

D EWEY W EBER (1938–1993), "the little man on wheels," was a gymnast and yo-yo champion, the original Buster Brown Kid, whose flamboyant antics on a surfboard defined the performance school known as hotdogging. He bought into the boom, became one of the biggest surfboard manufacturers, and died at fifty-four of liver failure in the back of his surf shop in Hermosa Beach, California.

P HIL E DWARDS (b. 1938), considered the best surfer in the world, at first by word of mouth through the infamous "coconut wireless," then as winner of the first Surfer Magazine Poll, eschewed the trappings of fame, although his first ride at the previously untried Banzai Pipeline was immortalized in the 1961 Bruce Brown film, *Surfing Hollow Days*. Like the great surfer and glider pilot Woody Brown before him, Edwards went on to design and build multihull boats, including the Hobie Cat.

Bob Simmons planing into the shorebreak at Malibu in the summer of '47

The surfers posed around this vintage woody at Makaha in December of 1962 are (left to right): unidentified, Ivan Vanetta, Frank Grannis, Paul Strauch, and two of the era's surf queens, Candy and Robin Calhoun.

John Severson

The Surfer

JOHN SEVERSON, INVENTING SURF CULTURE

The sun slips behind the Hawaiian island of Moloka'i, spilling a jeweled gore of red-sand oranges across the channel, smearing streaks of cloud with tropic fire. Swells blacken and lift near the corners of the cove at Honokeana as the classic beach house on the lava point is warmed by the dying of another Maui day. Below the house, an Angulo longboard sits on the grass, still beaded with the salted pearls of an afternoon session. A sizable wooden deck is a grand platform from which to view all of this. ❧ Inside the house, a large man with big hands and feet and lively blue eyes sits beneath a painting of a deserted hillside golf green with perfect waves wrapping into Honolua Bay below. He wears shorts and a bright Hawaiian

Still jazzed in the juice, John Severson cuts back at Thousand Peaks, near his home in West Maui, 1998

37

SURFING MOVIE

John **SEVERSON** PRESENTS

"SURF FEVER"

All New 1960 Color Surfing Adventure filmed in HAWAII • CALIF • MEXICO and NEVADA !

— SPECIAL ADDED SHOWING —

PACIFIC BEACH JR. HIGH AUD.

shirt and appears to be reading the novel *Gidget Must Die.* Perched in the loft above, a bronze Buddha casts a meditative calm down on bamboo furniture, woven rattan floor mats, shell-encrusted lampshades, an evocative miscellany of Hawaiiana. The place exudes the aesthetics of surf art, incarnate.

Severson came here to Maui back in the early 1970s. He built this house twenty-five years ago. Framed with eucalyptus poles, sheathed in shingles, it's as perfect in this setting as the grass shacks and pole houses of his painted tropical fantasies. The whimsical curves and angles of the Polynesian-style roof, the Hobbit-hole nuances of the windows, the casual but graceful use of space, the balanced feng shui of the set and setting—all of this reflects Severson's prodigious creative gifts and his restless imagination.

JOHN HUGH SEVERSON WAS BORN IN LOS ANGELES, California, in December of 1933. His father worked in the rationing-encumbered service-station industry until he bought his own station in San Clemente and moved his family to the beach in the fall of '45. Severson was stand-up surfing by the time he was fourteen, and then he saw a copy of Dr. John Ball's 1946 book, *California Surfriding,* and his fingers started to fidget. "There was a little picture of a letter a guy had written during the War, back to the Santa Cruz guys, and he drew a picture of a wave or a surfer or something. That really struck me, and I started cartooning."

In 1951, Severson got a Malibu "chip" surfboard—a Joe Quigg design that felt so light and tippy that he and younger brother Jimmy never thought

Severson and his daughter,
Jenna, posed for *Life* magazine
cameras in 1964.

they'd be able to ride it. About this time, Severson fell under the influence of the so-called Pasadena Playboys, a bunch of partyers who would show up in San Clemente in the summer. "They'd come down and play two-man volleyball," Severson tells me, "and they'd bring their little sisters. It was just perfect! They opened new worlds for us."

Severson was a high-school athlete, loved baseball especially, and pitched until his arm blew out. A teacher suggested alternatives—band, the school paper, wood-block prints, art, and more. He excelled in all. He pumped gas in winter and worked as a lifeguard in summer, graduated, got an associate's degree from Orange Coast College, went inland (California State University, Chico) to earn a degree in art education, then started working on his master's at California State University, Long Beach, in the fall of '55. There, he surfed, drank beer, sang barbershop, and got into a painting class taught by Dr. John Olson, who told Severson to "paint what you have fun doing."

"So I started a picture of the pier," Severson tells me. "I'm very tight and linear. I'm palette-knife painting because I'm a little fearful of laying out my brushwork in front of the whole painting class." Olson was enthused by the subject matter, but his classmates weren't. "They just didn't dig it. But I couldn't be budged." Severson painted another one and took it to a gallery in Laguna Beach, where it sold right away for thirty-five dollars. Encouraged, he painted another—"a surf car with these funky little guys, boards loaded on top, and the faint representation of a wave. You could almost feel 'em boogyin' along. . . ."—and it sold within a week for $150.

Severson found himself in a wonderful dream. Being able to merge his creative spirit with his predilection for surfing and his love of waves was a revelation. At school, he attacked the canvas with every sort of experiment, looking for the language that would best communicate a choice slice of southern California life that no one seemed to notice or appreciate. The result was *Seal Beach Locals*, his first bona fide surf-culture painting; fittingly, he traded it for a new surfboard.

Severson earned his master's, scored a cherry teaching job, rented a little place in South Laguna, and carved a tiki to appease the ocean gods. Obligingly, the surf pumped all through that summer of '56, and Severson steamed into the school year with a big grin on his face, until one day in the mailbox: "Greetings! Drop everything and come with us."

Welcomed into the U.S. Army, he was sent to Colorado for basic training, where he got frostbite and was assigned indoors. "They set me up in a studio, painting and doing chain-of-command charts, during basic training! I was not a popular soldier." Moved to Georgia to learn teletyping and Morse code, his permanent assignments alternated between Germany and Hawaii. Some guy up the list

Severson met Louise Stier on the sidewalks of Waikiki in 1959. They've been together ever since.

In 1966, the staff of *Surfer* magazine included (left to right): Severson, Skip Newell, Pat McNulty, Don Thomas, Ron Dahlquist, Leo Bestgen, and Ron Stoner.

flunked out, and that's how Severson wound up in Honolulu in the spring of '57. This was a lucky man!

Stationed at Schofield Barracks, Severson was tasked with hand-tinting wall-sized topographical maps of Oahu in a beautiful open-air office. He rented a fifteen-dollar room in Waikiki, painted in the evenings, and sold his works on the sidewalk in front of the Royal Hawaiian hotel. The situation became a springboard for his career as a lifelong surfer and the single most important voice in the creation of twentieth-century surf culture. In Hawaii, he met the world's best surfers and surfed the world's best surf spots, and then he decided on his next creative project, a film.

Joe Quigg had moved to Honolulu in '53. "I first met John when I'd walk up and down Kalakaua," he recalls. "There was a hedge in front of the Moana hotel, and he'd sit there and sketch scenes of Waikiki and stuff, and I'd stop and chat. I loved him right from the start because his work was happy and colorful. Then he got a movie camera and made a movie, and to my mind that movie was a turning point in surfing."

Big-wave surfer Fred Van Dyke was also impressed. "John and his friend Ed Voss did things on the beach—they picked up litter, built designs in the sand, made sculptures of found objects. This was unique at the time, especially at Haleiwa beach, where the locals didn't appreciate outsiders. One time John and his friends made a Christmas tree out of driftwood with ornaments of junk—simple, but a creation in itself. John was certainly not rich at the time, but I think he enjoyed basking in being a poor person. He had the intellect and the artistic creativity, but he seemed to enjoy groveling in the surfer image."

Severson painted his car, transforming it into rolling surf art. As he traveled around Oahu checking the different surf spots, he filmed the action with an old sixteen-millimeter Keystone movie camera. He was there when the big swell of January '58 hit, ready with a roll-and-a-third of film. On the morning of the big day, Severson paddled out at Makaha with Buzzy Trent, had one great twenty-five-foot point-to-bowl ride with Trent, then dropped into a monster thirty-five footer, got drilled, saw the face of God, and blacked out several times before he could get a breath. He almost didn't survive, but as soon as he made it to the beach, he set up his camera.

Severson had a ball creating his first surf flick, framing its episodes in simple animations and hand-lettered titles, selecting the music. He called it *Surf.* It premiered at Honolulu's Roosevelt High School with Van Dyke narrating (Severson's stage fright kept him from narrating it himself) and was well received, and Van Dyke showed it around California the following summer.

When Severson mustered out of the Army in August, he was faced with either live-narrating the film or getting out of the business. Deciding to take the stage, he wrote and rehearsed the script, ran through the film repeatedly, practiced day and night, and when it came the night of the first show, "it was some funky little social hall—only 125 people or something—and I panicked."

He offered up a convenient bail-out line, "You didn't come to hear me talk, so let's have the lights and the action," and suddenly the place was dark. "I had this horrible realization . . . that the lights went out on my script, too!" Severson roars. "I couldn't believe it! All my best-laid plans!" But as the film rolled on, Severson found his voice. "It was so easy! I hadn't been counting on picture-word association. And over time, things got better. I learned a lot about timing, and how the audience is really just one person."

Severson's 2000 watercolor *End of the Road* depicts the surfer's search for a perfect place with perfect waves.

The money he got from *Surf* went into new equipment and a second film, *Surf Safari.* It was 1959, the year Columbia Pictures released *Gidget,* starring Sandra Dee as "the little girl with the big ideas" and Cliff Robertson as Kahoona, the bum with the beach shack. Dick Dale had taken up surfing and was beginning to work it into the music he made with his group the Del-Tones. Young people were flocking to the coast. "Surf City, USA" was under construction.

The interior of Severson's Maui beach house, a house Severson built himself, reflects his artistic sensibility and the surfer style he helped to popularize.

Severson met Louise Stier at the hedge in Waikiki when she was a student at the University of Hawaii. He met her again at a showing of *Surf Safari* in San Francisco. On December 4, 1959, Severson and Stier were married in Honolulu. That year he shot his third film, *Surf Fever* (the film he rates as his best). He was painting less; his art form was becoming cinematography. In addition to the movies, he burned four thirty-six-exposure rolls of black-and-white film over the winter of 1959–60, sometimes setting up his still camera next to the Bolex.

He used the stills and "frame grabs" from the film in a magazine-like booklet he sold to movie patrons for $1.25. He called it *The Surfer,* and it featured the same unique hand-lettering style he'd developed for his movies along with bits of the wit and wisdom he'd accumulated in his first twenty-six years of life.

Thus began *The Surfer* magazine. Later it was *Surfer Bi-Monthly,* then simply *Surfer.* It was a good wave, and Severson rode it well. Juggling magazines and movies and then family as well, he interpreted a dispersed, outlaw subculture in a way that both exposed and sanitized it, but also birthed it into an entity that has become, ultimately, one of the most meaningful of meaningless pursuits on this substantially blue planet. While the magazine provided a vehicle for his own creative powers, Severson was careful not to monopolize it; instead, he let it become a forum for surfers to do what they do best, which is, basically, show off and have fun.

"So Severson comes along and makes a movie," says Quigg. "It's got kids on small waves having the time of their life on the beach, and all that, and I really feel strongly that he changed the direction of surfing. And when he came out with his magazine, I loved that—getting kids laughing and having a good time. He broke that macho–killer barrier. I've always looked up to John because I feel he brought on the change and let kids dominate the sport."

Ten years down the line, Severson "bailed" on *Surfer.* He'd had enough of magazines and advertisers and the southern California boom he was so much a part of. He saw the writing on the wall when Richard Nixon bought the shoreline estate next door and renamed it the Western White House.

"I was surfing alone one day, and Nixon was sunning on the beach and watching. I surfed in, a really smooth wave with lots of turns and off the lips, right to shore. There was a moment when I thought I might as well walk up and sit down and talk to him. I would tell him to stop the war. But in a flash, I realized it would be futile; he was just a cold-fish politician. So I gave him the head and eyebrow raise, and he nodded back, and I moved on to another world."

Severson made one last, good film—*Pacific Vibrations,* a cautionary tale of surfing in those challenging times—then sold the business, moved to Maui, traveled along some backwaters not too far from the heart of darkness, and finally found an enduring life of artful existence on this south-facing shore.

Now, in 1999, I sit in his house and marvel at this man's achievements, at the sheer quantity of beauty for which Severson has been personally responsible. It's utterly amazing—not only his personal production of films, photographs, fabric designs, magazines, homes (he's built his last three), books, drawings, paintings, and wonderful lessons in prose—but the enormous beauty created by the many who have been inspired by him.

I ask him about any spiritual understandings he's come to about his art and surfing and this life.

"I don't know," he sighs. "The farther along I get and the more I think about it, the less I think about it. I've come to a center and feel very comfortable where I am, in my relationships with the family, and better about relationships with

Severson pulling block prints in his home studio

people. I am comfortable. But I think there's a great mystery about all of this. It's so amazing—everything put together in pieces and yet you can see through it all. It's very mysterious to me. I don't know where we're going. I see there's so many ways to look at it, and when people try to articulate it, they get in trouble and they start fighting about it, and a long time ago I decided it wasn't something you wanted to fight about. So, I just go along, and I'm ready for the big sleep, or I'm willing to go farther. Y'know, I'm ready to cruise to the next step."

He laughs his great young laugh, and his blue eyes dance beneath the gaze of the Buddha. Here he sits, the man who established the archetypes, who carved the icons on our collective consciousness, who synthesized the experiences of the surfers before him into a vision of surfing as a culture of art in action, where beauty can be found in every move, in every nuance of shifting life, and reality merges with fine art in the sanctuary of God's folding extravagance—the curling wave.

While taking time off from shooting *Pacific Vibrations* in 1969, Severson found transitional housing in the barrel of a wave at Pupukea on Oahu's North Shore.

Richard "Dick" Brewer and Gerry Lopez, defining and refining their state-of-the-art dream vehicles on the North Shore in the midst of the shortboard revolution, 1969

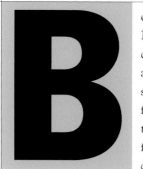**B**efore European contact, Hawaiians approached the constructing of a surfboard as a ritual. Everything—from the selection of the tree and its felling and preliminary carving to its transport, final shaping, finishing, and launching—was done in a cohesive community framework. The resulting surfboard was a family's prized possession.

In the absence of a supporting social structure, surfboard construction in the early twentieth century had become a much more pragmatic act. But it was still highly personalized, with most surfers shaping and finishing their own boards at the beach. In fact, making your own surfboard was an important aspect of being a waterman. All that changed in the 1930s, though, when Tom Blake's "genuine and approved" hollow boards began to be manufactured by the Thomas N. Rogers Company of Venice, California. These were the first "production" surfboards, and it was possible for anyone anywhere to buy one.

Over time, a special status evolved for surfers who could shape good surfboards, and the ability to do so translated into the first viable surf-related careers. By the '50s, several of California's top surfers had gone into business shaping boards for other surfers. In the process, they created jobs for fiberglassers, sanders, polishers, sales people, foam manufacturers, and more.

Surfboard design came down to interpreting the interplay of form and function, and function was related to the perceived goals of the surfer, and the goals of the surfer could change, depending on conditions or personal style. For some, however, there remained a mystical element at the core of the process of creating a surfboard.

In the early '60s, surfboards were still big (nine to ten feet long, generally) but increasingly lightweight and maneuverable. The men who shaped them had refined their art considerably since the days of Blake and Simmons; they had developed specialized boards for particular waves. Long, sleek "elephant guns" were used for the big Hawaiian winter surf, and big, wide "nose-riders" were all the rage in California's smaller stuff.

Hawaiian-born David Nuuhiwa was master of the nose-ride. Thanks to the shape of his surfboard (kick in the tail for "stickiness" and drag, a subtle concave under the nose for planing) and a knack for subtle unweighting and body English, he could stand on the front and "hang ten" (toes) over the tip for up to ten seconds. He was widely heralded as the world's best.

However, in '65, Santa Barbara, California, surfer George Greenough traveled to Australia with a new wave-riding vehicle he'd created, one that he rode on his knees. Short, scooped-out like a spoon, and foiled back to a thin, flexible tail (and a deep fin inspired by the dorsal of a tuna), "Velo" was a pure carving machine that redefined the available topography of a wave. After watching Greenough power-surfing his hypermaneuverable "neutral-handling" kneeboard, Australian shaper Bob McTavish sawed two feet off his own surfboard and launched the "shortboard revolution."

An aggressive surfer with a powerful style, Australian Nat Young triumphed over Nuuhiwa's more elegant nose-riding approach to win the '66 world championships in San Diego. As the number-one test pilot for the new V-bottom shortboards, Young was the spearhead of the revolution. By '70, there was scarcely a "longboard" in use anywhere in the surfing world, and people like Phil Edwards, Gidget, and Tom Blake were all but forgotten. Meanwhile, Vietnam was on fire, and surfers were heading for the hills.

Richard Brewer

Cheap Kensho

RICHARD BREWER, THE SHAPER'S WAY

Richard Brewer lives near Hanalei, about a mile upcountry from the highway on a flat five-acre prairie parcel darkly backed by the twin towers of Kaua'i's highest mountains, Kawaikini and Wai'ale'ale. The wettest area on earth is up there. The house is a white-stuccoed, two-story structure down a palm-lined hundred-yard drive past a similar but more flamboyant home. He and his wife Sherry live upstairs. 〰 Downstairs, exquisite shaped blanks are stacked on a sofa, ready for boxing. A glassed Brewer longboard lies on the carpet. The huge closet holds an array of Clark Foam shipping boxes (up to full-gun size), rolls of bubble pack, tape and other shipping materials, and a stack of business cards featuring a plumeria lei around the handwritten words "Dick

Surfboard designer and
shaper Dick Brewer, 1995

49

Brewer Surfboards" and, beneath the lei, "Hawaii." Bundled sets of thruster fins are spread out on the bar. Photos and articles from surf magazines crowd the mirror behind the bar.

Around the corner is another room. When you step into it and close the door, you could be anywhere: flat-black walls, brilliant fluorescent tubes, piles of foam dust, more photos, surfboard order forms with their generic outlines, a rack of rough-shaped blanks on one wall, Masonite templates hanging below a rack of glistening-white finished shapes on the other . . . a shiny, well-used planer resting on a stool as if cooling. This is where Dick Brewer performs his magic.

Upstairs in the small living room, the balsa "towboard" he shaped for Laird Hamilton to ride the largest waves ever ridden is mounted on the wall above the sliding glass doors that open out onto the covered porch, where we sit on soft chairs, sip juice squeezed from just-picked Key limes, and talk about Brewer's life and career. It's July 31, 1998.

Now past sixty, thicker and white-haired, but with a razor sharp recall for the telling detail, Brewer remains one of surfing's most contradictory characters. At once vague and precise, pragmatic but philosophical, self-absorbed and spiritual, he looks to have come a long, hard way from the famous David Darling photograph of him in lotus posture, with protégés Reno Abellira and Gerry Lopez at his side.

That photo was taken in '68. At the time, Brewer had emerged as the only viable opposition to a coup d'état of surfing being perpetrated by a small band of Australian rebels. While the American "surf industry" rocked back on its heels as their short vee-bottom boards swooned the surfing world, frantically retrenching and retooling to accommodate sudden shifts in function, fashion, and philosophy, Brewer assimilated and translated the new directions into his own evolving vision of the modern surfboard.

To the average surfer, at each stage of its evolution, the modern surfboard seemed a relatively done deal. But for the surfboard shapers who have navigated the sport through its evolution, it's always been about pushing the physical towards, the ideal, making what *might* be possible *actually* possible. Fired by

Brewer sliding under the lip at Pupukea, North Shore, on New Year's Eve, 1965

these evolutionary sentiments, from the day he first picked up a planer, Brewer gravitated toward the leading edge and surfing's ultimate specialty product—the big-wave "gun."

RICHARD ALLEN BREWER WAS BORN IN Bemidji, Minnesota, in 1936, but he grew up in California, where his machinist father worked at Douglas Aircraft. They lived on the shore in Long Beach, and Brewer loved the ocean. When the family moved to nearby Whittier for a time, he mowed lawns (including the Nixons) and worked around his father's machine shop. A lover of engines and fast cars, he hobbied at dragsters and high-performance model planes, but the waves were a relentless attraction, and after a stint as a college student and nightshift tool maker, he decided to try his hand at shaping a surfboard. He traced out a Quigg balsa board on one of Harold Walker's new foam blanks and made himself a 9'10" gun. "I shaped it in a garage in Surfside—that would have been about '59—and then I took my first trip to Hawaii, and it was all over."

Brewer was quick to establish himself on the North Shore of Oahu. He was fearless—took off on big set waves at Waimea Bay and jacking northwest peaks at Sunset Beach. A goofy-foot (right foot forward in his stance on the board) and not all that big, he'd go shoulder to shoulder with anyone out there, from Pat Curren to Greg Noll. Credibility in the water helped build credibility on the beach, and his future came into focus. "I decided not to become an aeronautical engineer," he recalls. "I decided it would be more fun to design surfboards." In the winter of 1960–61, Brewer opened Surfboards Hawaii, the first surf shop in Haleiwa.

Setting up shop on the North Shore put Brewer in the center of the prestigious big-gun action and on an accelerated learning curve. Gifted with his craftsman's hands, Surfboards Hawaii was soon a prestigious label, and Brewer seemed poised for long-term success. But then he entered into a licensing agreement that allowed boards to be made under the Surfboards Hawaii name in California, and through some sleight of hand involving "holographic contracts" he ended up losing the brand.

Sitting on the porch, watching red-headed cardinals flutter around in the fruit trees, Brewer could recall a litany of similar disappointments over the years. Certainly he has not been able to achieve the financial success of many of his contemporaries,

Brewer with his number-one test pilot, Reno Abellira. Oahu, 1969

most lesser-known and more minor contributors to the evolution of the surfboard and to surf culture. "I should have studied law, not engineering," he quips.

He walked away from Surfboards Hawaii and went to work for Hobie Surfboards in Dana Point, California, in '65, serving a genuine apprenticeship in production shaping with powerhouse machines Ralph Parker and Terry Martin, who, says Brewer, once shaped eighty-nine surfboards in a single week (the average shaper does about ten to twenty per week). After that, Brewer moved on to Harbour Surfboards of Seal Beach, California, Bing Surfboards of Hermosa Beach, California, and a few other outfits before heading back to Hawaii, this time to Kaua'i, where he set up shop in the small village of Hanapēpē. He got a deal designing and shaping lightweight guns for Bing through Fred Schwartz's Surfline Hawaii outlet in Honolulu.

By the summer of '66 and the run-up to the world championship contest in San Diego, Brewer's rising status was reflected in Bing's magazine spreads, which featured top competitor David Nuuhiwa and Brewer as star-power equals in a unique surfer-shaper relationship that was producing the new lightweight Pintail and Lotus surfboards. But Brewer preferred being his own boss. Over the years, he had developed a crew of loyal test pilots, and now they were on to something new.

"RB had pretty good antennae for seeing who was good and coming up and on the cutting edge," says Jeff Hakman, who won the '65 Duke Kahanamoku Invitational on a Brewer. "He hung with the younger guys, and there was a lot of smoking joints, and LSD was the mode, so he clicked right in with the surfers. Greg Noll had his team, and Hobie too, but RB's was just light years ahead—the hottest, most innovative guys, and he was always thinking, asking his riders, 'What about a board with more of a low rail and edge up front?' and then, 'What about shorter boards?'"

That was the vision: smaller, lighter, pintail surfboards that could ride high and tight up inside the curl of a hollow Hawaiian wave. "When we got into the mini-gun thing, we just took it on our own," Brewer recalls. "I went out and got a

Opposite: The famous "lotus" photo session of '68 captured shaping guru Brewer in meditation with "students" Gerry Lopez (left) and Reno Abellira in a little park below Mt. Tantalus. The building was a Honolulu water-supply pumping station. The image defined an era.

whole bunch of reject blanks, and me and Jeff Hakman and Jock Sutherland and Gary and Owl Chapman—we'd work all night building and glassing these fantastic boards, then we'd go to Mexico, or Rincon [in Santa Barbara] if it was winter time, or we'd go back to Maui with these boards with colors all over 'em."

Clearly they had new inspiration. "This was during the acid era, right? Bing fired me for 'putting his shop in disorder,' so the whole bunch of us split to Maui, and that's when Lahaina Surfing Design started." The initials said it all: LSD. It was a time of unparalleled creative development, and Brewer was tuned into what the young surfers wanted—"pocket rockets."

As the big bang of the wide-tailed vee-bottom surfboards faded, the sophistication of Brewer's shapes, ridden by inspired young surfers, brought validity and increasing momentum to the pocket-rocket approach. Although plenty of the big-wave riders still rode his guns, in a period of lessened big-wave focus, Brewer was able to hold his position as a dominant force in the surfing world, yet still he continued to have problems. Maybe it was arrogance, maybe it was drugs, and maybe it was a combination of being in high demand and seeing the arrogance of others.

Brewer had cast his lot for independence, but what this meant was an ongoing series of business relationships, some that worked and some that didn't. The LSD shop closed up in '68; he had a short run with Plastic Fantastic, a Hawaii-California surf company that had strong associations with the drug scene; and in '69, Brewer and Abellira became involved with the Gordon & Smith label, Inter-Island surfboards. After that, having essentially established himself as a shaper-for-hire, Brewer retreated to Kaua'i, where he would spend much of the next decade in virtual seclusion, going through good times and dark times while the evolution of the modern surfboard continued. He brought Gerry Lopez ("his best student") over to join him in the shaping room at his Hanapēpē shop. Brewer credits Lopez with teaching him yoga. It was also in Hanapēpē that Brewer met the priest who showed him the way of Zen, which led to the "white light."

"You know, I didn't really trip out as much as a lot of people," he tells me. "My first acid trip was when Butch Van Artsdalen had some vials of 'purple hat' Owsley, so me and Jackie Eberle dropped and paddled out at Waimea Bay. For the first year of the psychedelic thing, that was what we all took when Waimea broke, or big Honolua Bay."

"A vile of acid then paddling out to surf at Waimea Bay? This is hard to imagine," I say.

"Well," he sighs, "you either find reality or you don't find anything. I saw Jackie Eberle lose it and never come back one time. And that's when I started

When experienced surfers are putting their lives on the line in huge surf, many go to Brewer for an absolutely reliable "tow board." Brewer with rider Titus Kinimaka in Hanalei, Kaua'i, January 2001

slowing down on the stuff. And that's what made me finally go to a temple with a real Buddhist priest, right here on this island. He told me, 'Mr. Brewer, just you come every morning at six o'clock. We sit.' And I came and sat for an hour every morning for a year with the priest in a little temple in a plantation town called Wahiawa. It's gone now. I drove from Hanapepe where my surf shop was, up the hill a couple miles to the temple every morning, and then I'd go surfing. It became a real religious thing.

"I became a vegetarian, and I was for six years. When I started this whole thing, I had a stooped back—I was bent over from shaping all those big guns. And at the end of it, after I went to *sesshin* with the Roshi on Oahu, my posture became very good, although the hunchback has tended to come back since then. Maybe I need more long-time sitting."

The leader of the *sesshin* was Yosefani Roshi, who is mentioned in *The Three Pillars of Zen*, the classic guide to Zen Buddhism written by world-renowned Buddhist teacher Roshi Kapleau. "I had this religious experience sitting there," Brewer remembers with a soft smile. "I was at the white light. It was very beautiful. Then, when they rang the bell—and they rang the bell every hour—everybody followed each other around the room, because you get into this state of consciousness where you're not even thinking, for days. And when the bell rang, a crack went through the beautiful white light. And I wanted back there. They said I started crying like a little baby. They heard me cry, and they went, 'A baby!' I wanted to be back there."

I can feel how he misses it—like an addict longing for his high, but different. "I remember when they brought me in to sit in front of the Roshi. He was sitting here right in front of me with this light garment on, and the wind was blowing, and he was like a python snake. He was so loose! His joints were just all stacked up on top of each other. Like they say, no tight muscles. Where the wind would blow his consciousness. And I was right there with him. Just for a short time. I'd flicker in and out of that consciousness. Maybe it only lasted a month, but I was there. I know I was."

"But it's gone away?" I ask.

"Yeah, but they want me to find enlightenment," he answers without apparent vanity. "They want *some* Western man to find it. To them, Alan Watts and Timothy Leary couldn't sit in front of the Roshi at a high level of consciousness like I did. To them I was the first Western man that had enlightenment, as far as they knew. This was the real deal, y'know what I mean?"

"They told you this?" I ask.

"*Yeah*. They weren't even sure that Western man could even get there. The priest that taught me, Khomi, said that you're born enlightened, that your parents hang you up. He made me aware that we don't have to go sit or do some *thing* to reach it, that all you can be is your self."

"Did you practice the sitting for long?" I ask.

"Till the wreck on Maui in '75. I never sat *zazen* after that."

It was a car crash. Brewer was driving; his second wife, Ann, and their son and daughter were in the car. Keoki, the son, was killed. Brewer wound up in the hospital with a badly busted-up leg and layers of wounds, from the skin on down to the soul.

"After the car accident, I spent two months in a room with a junkie," he remembers. "They put me on morphine, and then they almost cut my leg off. There were thirty-some major pieces of bone, and they weren't healing. I could feel the bone pieces, so I told 'em to shoot me up with morphine so I could push 'em around, and after a while the X rays showed it was turning white between the bones. Anyway, this junkie saw me withdrawing from the morphine and had me snorting China white, and he brought me down slowly with that.

"It fixed my leg, but I got strung out," he admits. "Then they let me out of the hospital, and—wouldn't you know it?—I ran into this guy on the street. Now I know that I'm an addictive person."

Brewer then spent several years in a kind of twilight underground. He went from doing his best work, from pioneering three-fin boards, stingers, twin fins, concaves, and just about everything else, to relative obscurity—living mostly on the North Shore, still shaping, but no longer near the center of things. He emerged again in the mid-'80s, when he learned to windsurf and began shaping sailboards. Then he met Sherry on an inter-island flight, and his life again took a turn.

"Women—the things they do," he smiles whimsically. "Hard to replace."

Now, a few years into it, he's back into the groove, making beautiful boards and weaning himself off the real-estate work that had helped him make the transition into this new place and time. He has a new business partner, an attorney in the wine business—Jess Jackson of Kendall-Jackson Wineries. "He's a very, very

Over forty years into it, Brewer remains one of the world's most respected shapers, building everything from longboards to tiny shortboard thrusters and the small, solid guns designed for the world's largest surf.

generous person," Brewer states, Brando-like. "Duke Kahanamoku taught him to surf back in the '50s. Jess has given me a lot of advice on how to do this thing. We have a new logo—it's the lei, and it's called Plumeria. We're starting out to work with Laird Hamilton, Darrick Doerner, and Buzzy Kerbox [all three are big-wave masters] on towboards with the Plumeria logo."

Towboards are small surfboards with foot straps—like waterskis or snowboards. They're ridden in giant waves—thirty to sixty feet—by watermen who are towed in by partners piloting jet-ski-style personal watercraft (PWCs). The sport can be life or death, so equipment is critical. That some of the very best tow-surfers are using his boards speaks volumes about the confidence they have in Brewer's wave-riding vehicles.

Here on Earth, it's all about Karma Yoga, and even Brewer has to mow the lawn. Note the "Shaping Guru" T-shirt.

Back on Brewer's porch, overlooking the fruit trees with the red flickering and chatter of cardinals, the conversation moves to the shaper's role in surfing. "Duke Kahanamoku came to my shaping room one time. It was 1967, and Jock Sutherland had won the Duke meet on a Brewer with the Duke label on it. He said he was very proud that one of his boards had won the Duke meet, and he said that in the old days a surfboard builder was considered a *kahuna.* He said, 'You have great powers, my son. Don't abuse your powers.'"

"So, if a shaper is a *kahuna,* you'd have to be a *kahuna,*" I point out.

"Which is considered a holy man in the Hawaiian culture. But I never tried to play that role," says Brewer. "My thing is, I'm not playing any role. I'm just a designer that's really interested in contributing to humanity. To still be communicating and contributing to humanity at this time in history makes my life worthwhile."

I ask him if he's ever considered another direction in his life.

"Yeah," he admits. "There was a time when I was studying Zen with my teacher, and I thought about going back into engineering or selling real estate . . . and I *am* a real estate broker. My teacher told me—and I didn't realize he realized all these things—he started talking about all these little things I'd done with fins and bottom curves and things, and he says, 'Mr. Brewer, this surfboard design thing, you must finish what you start.' And this was one of the few pieces of advice that I got from a real Zen person—that, since I started this surfboard design thing, I must finish it."

Curl upon curl in the Waimea Bay
shorebreak, December 1978

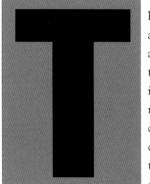he beach is a no man's land and a borderland, a desert and a wasteland. Not only the meeting of land and sea, it's the place where human-made law and order meet divinely organized chaos. For centuries (but especially in the last hundred years), this energetic nexus has served as a convenient escape for people fleeing the pressures of society, a gathering place where folks could let their hair down, breathe deeply, squeal with delight, get naked, or whatever.

"To live outside the law you must be honest," sang the poet Bob Dylan, and nature does have a way of keeping you honest. Reflecting its territorial playground, surf culture is anarchic. Not in the sense of disorder, per se, but in the sense of a "voluntary and cooperative association of individuals and groups as the principal mode of organized society" (*The Random House Dictionary of the English Language*). The presence of the ocean and its complexly chaotic yet lawful effects on the activity of surfing imbue the entire culture with the lessons learned in the surf. And these are perceived by surfers as superior and certainly more objective than "the law of the land."

"Like mos' stuff," Kelly, a beachboy, explains to a female tourist he's about to bed in James A. Michener's *Hawaii*, "surfin's gotta have its own rules."

The social criteria of the modern surfing subculture has been seeded with (and by) fundamental Polynesian values, which regarded surfing as noble, positive, and saturated with spiritual meaning. Modern surfing has a rich history, a unique system of rituals, distinctive language and symbolic elements, tribal social hierarchies, and other unique lifestyle characteristics, all of which have been broadly imitated and emulated around the world. Witness the "shaka" hand gesture (extended pinky and thumb), praying for surf, rules of the road at surf spots, hierarchical protocols at all notable beaches, honoring of subcultural elders, related lifestyle clothing industry, and a specialized language that gives esoteric meanings to common terms such as "green room," "stoke," "shack," "A-frame," "rip," "session," and "strapped."

At significant surf spots, the structure, rules, and strength of the local hierarchy control activity within the territory. All surfers know this. Every time we venture into a new surf spot and test a new territory, we enter into a "force field" of hierarchy. This field might be highly organized or it could be extremely anarchic; either way, you can bet there's an organizing paradigm, and every newcomer has to "get with it."

There's a sign—actually four wooden boards— near the stairs down to the water at Steamer Lane in Santa Cruz, California. On each board is written a rule:

- First surfer on wave has right of way.
- Paddle around wave not through it.
- Hang on to your board.
- Help other surfers.

Erected by old-school surfer Sam Reid and other devotees of a mid-twentieth-century waterman's ethic,

these previously unwritten rules evince an invisible binding force that held surf culture together in the pre– and post–World War II eras. That force has to do with respect and a shared sense of responsibility for one another and for surfing.

As each advancement in surfboard design calls forth new techniques and levels of performance, similarly (and often synchronously) each new era or generation needs to reinterpret and reintegrate surfing's history into its collective consciousness, gathering the material that brings context and meaning to its ephemeral pursuits.

As each step forward conducts the electricity of new expression through the armature of the ever-recurring field of energy we know as ocean waves, respect is what keeps the territory and the hierarchy properly aligned. Responsibility maintains and conducts the kind of positive energy that gave surfing its considerable allure in the first place. An atmosphere of responsibility and respect creates a matrix for the fun and challenging interaction with nature that draws us to riding waves.

The ability of surfers to withstand punishing big-wave situations was redefined with the discovery of the savage curls at Teahupo'o (pronounced *cho-poo*). The Fijian break, first ridden in 1985, was popularized in the 1990s and demonized in 2000, after it took the life of a local surfer. Here, a Teahupo'o macker chases Malik Joyeau over a razor-sharp coral bed.

Finalists at the 1965 world contest in Peru were (left to right): Nat Young, Nipper Williams, Mickey Muñoz, Mike Doyle, Paul Strauch, Fred Hemmings, George Downing, and Felipe Pomar, who won the event and the first official world title.

Nat Young

Animal Tracks

Nat Young, Tribal Elder

In March of 2000, five-time world champion surfer Nat Young was beaten to a pulp by a local bully named Michael Hutchinson, while surfing his local spot at Angourie in New South Wales, Australia. Hassled and badmouthed by Hutchinson's son, Luke, a celebrated wave hog, Young reportedly backhanded the sassy brat, thus setting off the old man, who'd already accumulated a considerable list of assaults (including two on police officers). Young's swollen mug—a portrait in vivid purples and oranges—appeared on the front page of the *Sydney Morning Herald* and other newspapers around the world, and it took hours of reconstructive surgery and plenty of titanium mesh to pull his face back together.

Nat Young was world champion in 1966, before going on, in a second competition career in the late '80s and early '90s, to become four-time world longboard champion.

I had spoken to Young by telephone a few times since the beating. Coming as it did on the heals of a severe head injury (snowboarding in Sun Valley, Idaho, in '94), I thought I was detecting some cracks in his armor, some signs that his enduring and sustaining positiveness had been damaged, perhaps permanently, by these two significant traumas. It was clear—after the head injury—that he took a while to get back into gear. His memory seemed affected, his speech somewhat slurred. It all sorted out eventually, but in the meantime, he had lost his lucrative and prestigious job as director of the Oxbow surfwear company's surf team. Then, after the beating, he seemed so utterly down and defeated—not by Hutchinson personally, but by the sheer stupidity of humankind—that I worried what would become of him.

So it was with some trepidation that I dashed through a sudden rain squall and into the lobby of Waikiki's Sheraton Princess Kaiulani Hotel late on a January afternoon, wondering if—after all that had occurred—I would even recognize him.

There in the lobby sat Ti, his wife, looking exactly as she had a decade ago. She wore a black dress and a big smile. Where was Nat? I asked. "Oh," she said, "he ran into some guy with a classic old Ford, and there was talk about going to some party up the way." A couple of minutes later, Young sauntered up out of the warm evening air, breezing into the lobby in a Hawaiian shirt, baggy pants, and sandals with his hair combed back in damp waves. He looked great. In fact, he looked

Left: Young enjoying a slice of watermelon in Peru, 1965, where he lost the world title match by one point to local hero Felipe Pomar

Above: Getting it done in Ocean Beach, California, Young rides "Sam" to victory in the 1966 World Surfing Championships

Right: Newly signed with the Weber surf team, Young joined Dewey Weber (left) for a groundbreaking session at Malibu in August of 1968.

exactly like Nat, and healthy except for a giant bulge on his left shoulder, a dislocation suffered while snowboarding at Fernie in British Columbia a few days earlier. It had capped off, as he put it, "the worst year of my life."

Young had come to Honolulu to promote *Surf Rage,* a volume of essays on the ugly underbelly of surfing. The book (a collection of perspectives by a range of writers from around the world) illustrates one of Young's cornerstone principles. "It's so easy for some people to say how lucky I have been throughout my life, how everything has come quite easily," he wrote in his introduction to the book. "I believe that is very simplistic and totally wrong. What I have achieved has come through paying attention to details and hard work, and the key to my success is that I have been very adept at turning negatives into positives."

BORN IN NOVEMBER OF 1947, Robert Harold Young spent his first years in the landlocked suburbs of western Sydney, but the family moved to the coast in '49, to a big old house overlooking the beautiful beach at Collaroy. There the lad learned to swim and ride waves on a surf-o-plane, the inflatable rubber mats popular in Australia in those days. At first so small and wiry they called him "The Gnat," the boy grew out of all proportion to his humble origins to become the greatest surfer of his time and an icon in the tradition of Kahanamoku, Blake, Edwards, and Dora.

Four greats of the era, (left to right) Young, Jock Sutherland, Rusty Miller, and Rick Grigg, head for the water and their heat in the 1968 Duke Kahanamoku Invitational Surfing Championships at Sunset Beach, Oahu

Young drives low to set up in the steepening inside section at Sunset Beach in the final of the '68 Duke contest

His magnetic enthusiasm and powerful style on shorter and shorter boards blew open the doors of a new era back in the mid-'60s. He was Australian national champion in '65, world champion in '66. By then, the six-foot-three-inch man with the size-thirteen feet had outgrown his diminutive nickname. He was Nat, but they called him "The Animal."

Despite the bestial moniker, Young was never exactly comfortable scrounging his way through life; he wasn't willing to live the low life to maintain the beach life. He was drawn to the best that life had to offer, and it (by that most fundamental law of alchemy) was drawn to him. Rather, tagging him "The Animal" was a tongue-in-cheek nod to Young's ambition, to his appetites and enthusiasm, to his unquenchable lust for life.

Surfing is a big slice of Young's life, and often it's what matters most. But not always. Surfing's the centerpiece of what he calls "a beautiful life." Indeed, Young, the self-styled icon and tribal elder, the author, publisher, filmmaker, teacher, lobbyist, fashion model, businessman, spokesperson, pilot, gourmand, instigator, theorist, philosopher (surfers *do* sometimes get wise), surfboard shaper, politician, adventurer, and skilled practitioner of surfing and other gravitational gratifications including skiing, snowboarding, river rafting, and windsurfing, is as much a man of the mind as he is a man of the body. His ongoing war, for over three decades now, has been with bullshit, a commodity with which he himself has occasionally been associated. His chief weapon (and general conversational style) has been brutal honesty, admittedly from his own subjective point of view. Still, few in surfing (or any other endeavor, for that matter) have so thoroughly and diligently pondered their purpose as has Young. And no one in surfing has taken on the mantle of educator, inspirer, enlightener, and leader the way he has. He's defined the role of a tribal elder so that he can fill it.

Young is a renaissance surfer who takes his role and its implications very seriously, who's pondered the nature of surfing in deeply existential explorations, who's considered its fundamental mechanics in the most basic terms, who's championed the preservation of the ocean environment and the preservation of the sport's history, who's considered to be one of the greatest surfers in that history, and who's still a damn good surfer at age fifty-five. It is further arguable that Young's continued mastery and championing of longboard surfing over the past decade has added a propulsive spiral to the continuing evolution of surfing.

Because Young has been outspoken in occasional interviews, articles, and books for over thirty years, most surfers have formed their opinions. Some love him, some hate him, some younger or newer surfers have never heard of him. "To be brutally honest," Young would likely comment, "I don't give a flyin' fuck."

A professional surfer from the start (he was already selling surfboards at fifteen, when he won a first-class round-trip airfare to Hawaii and California in the

Australian championships), he's got strong opinions about his career. "One of the best things I learned out of surfing was how to be a professional person," he tells me. "I suppose that means being on time. When you give your word, you're there."

Even so, Young's been an advocate for the judicial use of marijuana since the late '60s, when he sampled the gamut of psychotropic substances in an era that tended to support and nurture their more positive and visionary effects. "I was a devotee of the fact that marijuana was extremely good for everyone, and that LSD was the *best* thing," he admits. "I was of the school of Timothy Leary. I believed pretty much everything I was being told. I don't know whether that's good or bad or whatever, but I was there on all that stuff." In the early '70s, while enjoying genuine celebrity status, he and his family withdrew into a back-to-the earth experiment that seeded the present status of Australia's Byron Bay area as a haven for alternative lifestyles.

Yet he managed his life so forthrightly that his public image has remained generally positive in Australia, despite a few well-publicized incidents involving weed and rude behavior. His fame remains huge. He ran for the New South Wales State Parliament in '86 on a pro-environmental platform and got forty-seven percent of the vote, enough to leverage his issues into new clean-water legislation. A self-professed student of life, he cites his friend Peter Garrett and members of Garrett's Australia-based band Midnight Oil as examples of other individuals who dropped out of school early and have managed to turn a negative into a positive.

"The only reason I never went back to school was because I was learning too much. I didn't have enough time," he states. "I suppose there *were* still things for me to learn there, but I can't think really what they were. I do have problems with writing skills and spelling and things like that. People wonder why I still don't type, and I say because I've taught myself to write longhand."

A strong man needs a strong woman. Young's first wife was a schoolteacher—like his mum, a sweet woman who didn't surf and probably got more than she bargained for out of the relationship. Ti, too, is a nonsurfer—strong, completely unpretentious, vegetarian, and the daughter of a Sydney book publisher

Young with his 5'6" board after winning his early-round heat at Bell's Beach during the 1970 world contest

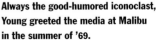

Always the good-humored iconoclast, Young greeted the media at Malibu in the summer of '69.

who took a few years off to educate his kids on long motorhome vacations in the United States and other parts of the world. Two children from Young's first marriage are now grown, and he and Ti travel together with their two younger ones—Australia, Idaho, Tahiti, Europe, Canada . . . it's all good.

"If there is sort of a story to me, it's that I was already on this path before I met Ti, and the fact that her father had died, but he left her with this principle and this way of living, which fitted absolutely with me, and we put all our channeled energy into that principle, and that principle applies very strongly to the children and what we're trying to do. And so far, for the last ten years, it hasn't really come off the rails at all because it's based on that. Make it a beautiful life."

"When did you and Ti get married?" I ask.

Young enjoying crisp, glassy conditions in Mexico in November of '79. Young's comprehension of waves is second only to his comprehension of human nature and the surfing subculture.

"I don't even *know*," he answers. "I don't ever *know* that stuff. I never know, and I almost don't care. All I know is that at some stage in all of this, when my body and my mind are no longer functioning as one, then I'm going to nip it in the bud and not be here anymore. And if I don't, then Ti will. And that was our only marriage vow."

"That she'll nip you in the bud?" I ask.

"Yeah, she'll get rid of me. I'm not going to be around being somebody that's looked after. I will not, and that's fine. I don't have any problem with that. I would assume it's somewhere around sixty-five, if I last that long."

SO WE CRAMMED INTO BEAR'S VINTAGE BEAST —a "classic" 1960 Chevy 327 Impala—Young and wife Ti, their daughter Nava, son Bryce, me, and a couple of friends Bear recognized on Kalakaua Boulevard, Waikiki's main drag. Then we headed out toward Diamond Head, looking for the party.

"The deal is," Young told me, "Gidget's gonna be there." It seemed Kathy Kohner was on the island to promote the reissue of her father's book.

On the way, Young raved and cracked jokes and grilled the driver, the hitchhikers, the universe at large. The style was refreshingly reminiscent of his witty raves on the North Shore years earlier. That we were being carriaged in the rusting hull of a vintage motorcar, perfumed by burnt oil squeezing past worn piston rings, only added to the atmosphere of acid flashback. I hoped the kids appreciated it.

Last time I saw Nava, she was about three feet tall; now she was twice that and had become a beautiful young woman. Bryce was busy incubating all the attitude of his dad and his older brother, Beau, the world's current longboard champion.

Turned out Bear was Bear Woznick, a highly accomplished practitioner of the newly rekindled art of tandem surfing. The well-muscled man was from Malibu and had come to the Islands to train for an upcoming event at Makaha. The party was at the house of Hawaii's hot tandem team, Kanani and Bobby Friedman, whose synchronized power surfing had lifted the once-stodgy art to new heights.

The real Gidget did indeed show up. She and Young immediately tangled in a fish ball of mutual flattery and praise while I gorged on the octopus sashimi.

Two evenings later, I picked up the Youngs at their hotel, and we scurried over to the Ala Moana harbor and the Charthouse restaurant, owned by surfing legend Joey Cabell, with whom Young had recently skied in Aspen.

Over dinner, Young reflected on the past ten months. Within a few days of the beating, even before the marathon reconstructive surgery, he had formulated the idea of publishing *Surf Rage* as a call to put an end to the snowballing violence at beaches around the world. Within a month, he was back in the water surfing, but the peace and contentment of living in Angourie had been shattered, and he and Ti decided to sell their holiday apartments there.

Less than two months after the beating, he had written the opening and closing chapters of his book and had assigned the other chapters to writers around the world. By June, he was off to the Australian Book Fair in Sydney flogging sales with sample chapters. In the aftermath of his Oxbow job, he put together a new deal with BIC Sports that inked in July. On his return to Australia in August, he stopped over in Cambodia, where Ti flew up to meet him and spend a few days touring the birthplace of Buddhism and the Khmer empire of Angkor Wat. He was home in Australia in time to carry the Olympic torch on its 500-meter leg through Byron Bay.

In August, he bashed his thumb with a hammer while doing some remodeling work on the apartments (bug-infested silky oak!). The book was completed by the end of that month, and by October *Surf Rage* was off the press in Singapore. Meanwhile, he was surfing with his kids whenever the waves were good, and his '98 biography, *Nat's Nat and That's That,* was selling out its second printing.

Typically, he said: "The time in the hospital recovering from the serious head wound was where I got into working on the book *Nat's Nat and That's That.* If it hadn't been for the time spent convalescing, I would never have been disciplined enough to sit down and write my autobiography in longhand."

In the aftermath of the Angourie punch-out, more than one surfer said that Young deserved what he got. After all, he has a reputation as an aggressive surfer who sometimes takes more than his share of the waves. So I asked him if he'd ever punched anyone over waves—had he ever lost it in a fit of "surf rage"?

"No one deserves what happened to me," he answered. "And just for the record, I have never punched anyone at the beach or in the surf."

After dinner, we walked over to where Cabell's Quigg-designed catamaran, *Hokule'a,* was tethered in its slip. We admired its erotically sculpted shape and roamed carefully over its minimal deckscape, while Young reminded me that surfer, shaper, and all-around surfing legend Mickey Muñoz had been lashed to its mast for several days after he'd been knocked out by a swinging boom in the vicinity of the equator during a savage typhoon. Muñoz screaming with pain in the howling wind is an enduring image in my imagination.

A few months later, I received an email from Angourie that in some ways summed up the beautiful life:

"Hi Drew,

"Thought I had better let you know that we went to see Dylan on Saturday night, outdoors in Ballina with 5,000 people. The band was so young and full of energy. It was amazing. We were twenty feet from the stage, dancing, rocking; it was one of the best concerts I have ever been to. So glad I took Nava, Bryce, Beau, Ti, Nyarie [a friend].

"What amazed me was they were all the same old poetic words that we have loved forever, but every one was put into a new treatment. I found it took me two verses of a song to realize what it was. He really gave me faith in getting old. The guy can obviously still get off on his music because he re-invents himself. That's what I like about going from long- to shortboard and back."

"Talk to you soon, Beau is coming, it's six feet and grinding!

"Nat xx"

Making it a beautiful life: Four-time longboard champion Young lounged on the beach at Makaha with his son, Beau, in November of '97. The younger Young won his own world longboard title in 2000.

The essence of the artform: American surfer Alex Knost poised on the nose, slicing under the lip at Tamarindo in Costa Rica in January of 2002.

t the onset of the 1970s, surfing (and Western culture at large) stood at a crossroads. For surfers, it was the question, "Is riding waves a sport or an art form?" The community was polarized. On the one side were the mellowed multitudes; optimistically soothed by the peace-and-love ethic of the '60s, many of them saw the future of surfing as a community of like-minded brothers and sisters enjoying the waves and the ocean in joyful celebration.

On the other side were the select few, the great surfers and the hungry outsiders, who saw surfing as a ladder to stardom and greatness or as a vehicle for simple domination. These were surfers who loved to compete, who took more than their share of the waves, and—yeah—who made a living showing off for the cameras. For them, the early '70s was a bleak time during which the money and much of the color seemed drained from a sport that had held so much fiscal promise before the shortboard revolution.

The creative explosion of the '60s turned Western societies upside down and inside out. The outlaw subculture of surfers, equipped with the materials and technology to translate all manner of thought-forms into toys and artifacts, was especially quick to take the bait and transform life's dynamic gameboard into something entirely different. One simple crack in the cosmic egg of the status quo, and . . . voilà!

Suddenly surfers rode small boards called pocket rockets, mini-guns, fish, darts, and needles . . . twin-finned, tri-finned, and keel-finned surfboards that related to waves in entirely new ways. Expanding the range of surfing performance went hand in hand with expanding your mind. Early devotees of psychedelics and other psychotropics, surfers were in the cultural vanguard of some of the period's most popular movements, from ecotourism and adventure travel to skateboarding, snowboarding, and various other so-called "extreme" sports.

In the renaissance spirit of "do your own thing," there were suddenly hundreds of so-called "underground" shapers, hell-bent on creating the ultimate surfboard, inspiring legions of local explorers to test the boundaries of the possible. The underground went deeper, of course, as the search for waves celebrated in Bruce Brown's film, *The Endless Summer* (1966), put ever more surfers on the road to world exploration and adventure, a lifestyle that many naturally parlayed into profitable sidelines.

The dominant surfers of this time represented the generational mind-set, but with idiosyncratic gifts for self-expression and experimentation. In their surfing, this emerged as a beautiful consciousness of flow. Instead of the foot-pedaling, nose-riding, and exaggerated twists and rotations of the longboard era, surfing at the highest levels was now about "experiencing" the ride, and there was often a pure and subtle sensualism in the highly nuanced wave-riding styles of the day.

As the '70s rolled on and money and media wedged deeper into the sport, a reactionary movement of "soul-surfers" resonated with the era's back-to-the-land Luddite sensibilities and followed a parallel course off the beaten path and into the more obscure surfing areas of the developed world and, increasingly, into new frontiers, where white men with surfboards were pretty much out of the ordinary.

Bill Hamilton

The Stylist

Nervously psyching up for his heat in the 1969 Duke Kahanamoku Invitational, Bill Hamilton keeps his eyes on the surf at Sunset Beach.

Past the back entrance into Princeville on the north shore of Kaua'i, near Hanalei, the pavement stops and the road goes dark as it burrows into mango and hau trees. Down about half a mile, I come to a lone gray, windowless, and unmarked building and park the car. Stepping out into the cool, mosquito-rich morning, the air is filled with sweet-and-sour tropic aromas and the familiar buzzing shriek of a planer. The door is open. Inside, the small building is divided into three or four rooms; in one of them, I find a masked John Rogers laying up fiberglass on one of Bill Hamilton's patented fabric-railed longboards. In the next room, I find Hamilton himself, in paper mask and foam dust, shaping a shortboard for one of his team riders. He glances up, shuts off the planer, pulls off the mask, and flashes a big grin.

I haven't seen much of Hamilton since the early-1970s, when he was living on the North Shore, right at Pipeline, and then here on Kaua'i. At the time, I regarded him as one of the most impressive surfers in the world, having pulled off a seamless transition from great longboard stylist to great shortboard stylist, a feat about as rare as silent-movie stars making it in the talkies. In fact, surfing a shortboard exposed Hamilton for what he really was—a very radical guy disguised as one of the sport's most genial and easy-going gentlemen.

The North Shore seemed to bring out the wild man in Hamilton; the competitor, too. He placed ninth in the '69 Duke Kahanamoku Invitational, then sixth in '70 and second in '71, when he was runner-up at the Smirnoff Pro-Am, too—all

events held at Sunset Beach, a spot he loved. He was also a more-than-credible performer in the Expression Sessions of '70 and '71 at Pipeline, but just when a serious professional career started to seem like a viable option, he pulled up stakes and moved here to Kaua'i.

By '73, he and his wife JoAnn and their two blond-haired boys, Laird and Lyon, were living in a little tin-roofed house alongside the road in the idyllic but dangerous nowhere-land beyond Hanalei Bay. He seemed stoked at the time, shaping a few boards, growing some herb, surfing uncrowded waves, enjoying a simple, relatively solitary life. In those years, his independent and adventurous spirit found voice in a poetic sensibility, which seemed to flow from a visionary but commonsense philosophy. I enjoyed reading the occasional piece by him in *Surfer* magazine.

Now, he tours me through his shop—glassing room, sanding room, finish room, shaping room, and a front room, with stacks of finished surfboards, tow-boards, the odd surf ski, and a small dusty office corner. The walls are covered with surf photos, stickers, letters from customers, phone numbers, job orders, and assorted memorabilia. One of the largest and most impressive images depicts his stepson, Laird, riding a pornographically huge wave at a spot on Maui called Jaws.

The story of his meeting with Laird is a true myth: After enjoying some spontaneous ocean play together in small waves near Hamilton's house, two-year-old Laird walked up to him and announced, "I want you to be my daddy," then took him by the hand and led him to his mother. Curiously, that first encounter with Laird presaged an uncanny replay of his own youth in the idyllic South Laguna Beach of the 1950s.

A DOUBLE-TRACK DIRT DRIVE, slick with wet leaves, rotting fruit, and the henna-red mud for which Kaua'i is so famous, leads down to the small house Hamilton shares with his wife, Rhonda. Off to one side, ramshackle structures shelter an assortment of lumber, bikes, car and boat parts, junk, surfboard blanks, and a foliage-covered '65 International truck, a "future restoration project." A few steps across the lawn is the languid, green water of the Hanalei River, which flows down from the misty mountain crags in veins of silver. There's a small gazebo there with a few chairs, a fine Spanish guitar, and a set of weights. That's where we sit in the afternoon shade and talk about Hamilton's life.

His father had an orchestra and played in ballrooms across the country in the 1930s and '50s. His mother was a watercolorist and a cello player, who came to the marriage with an infant son, Gordon. They moved West, where William Stuart Hamilton was born in August of 1948, and lived in South Laguna, a paradise on earth in those days. The beach between Eighth and Eleventh Streets was a play-ground for Hamilton and his older, more world-wise stepbrother, and there was plenty of adventure in the coastal canyons, too. Tagging along with Gordon, he learned to hunt, fish, and scavenge, and forage on Laguna's richly populated reefs. Gordon later became a Hell's Angel; along with everything else, he taught his brother how to defend himself.

Hamilton liked hunting octopus at low tide. "You'd find 'em in holes on the flat part of the reef," he says. "I'd reach into the hole, let the octopus grab me, and pull 'em out. But this one time, I reached in and it grabbed me, and I tried to pull it out, but it wouldn't come, and it wasn't letting go, and the tide was coming up. His tentacles had gone up my arm, and they're holding me, and I can't get away. I'm really scared. The tide is up to my chin. I'm gonna drown. And then I relax . . . and the thing lets go of me."

Peace. Hamilton paddles back out after a wave at Silver Channels, at Mokuleia Bay on Oahu, 1969

Creative and dynamic at every turn, Hamilton's surfing was at its peak in the early shortboard era. Here he ducks under the end pitch of a tasty Velzyland looper on the North Shore, 1969

Art and celebrity were part of their Laguna Beach community. "Rock Hudson would bring his boyfriend down, and they'd oil each other all over," Hamilton laughs. "And that old fag Sterling Halloway, who wrote *Somewhere Over the Rainbow,* he had a house right above my house." Two visitors from La Jolla introduced Hamilton to the wonders of flamenco guitar. Even before high school, the boy had been strongly influenced by Dale Carnegie's *The Power of Positive Thinking* and Thoreau's poems on man and nature. "I was interested in religion when I was younger," he says, "religion in the sense of meditation."

Hamilton's spontaneous maneuvers in the early years of the shortboard era helped define the creative trajectory of the era—it was all about the freedom to go wherever you wanted. Punching through the lip at Pipeline, 1969

In the mid '50s, Hamilton came into the orbit of Dick Pettit and Joyce Van Every, an athletic and rather bohemian couple. "They were young, vibrant people who had an A-frame on the beach; it was just like Tahiti in the summertime. They had a *palapa* and a Tahitian bungalow . . . there was always a hammock. She painted Popeye cartoons, and he worked for a fiberglass company." They were water people, too, and Hamilton spent countless days with them, swimming and diving, fishing and riding waves. Joyce became Hamilton's surrogate mother. "She was absolutely gorgeous," he says. "I had a huge crush on her."

He bought his first surfboard from Van Every in '59, a blue Hobie; the following year Pettit and Van Every started taking him on surf trips—Dana Point,

Baja, and sometimes up to Rincon. He rode waves with the great surfers of the day: Dora, Edwards, and Van Artsdalen, in addition to Mike Doyle, L.J. Richards, Johnny Fain, Skip Frye, the Patterson Brothers, and more. He attempted to integrate what he learned from them into his surfing; what emerged was a style with its own artful panache. His own buddies, including Corky Carroll, Herbie Torrens, and Mark Martinson, jokingly characterized Hamilton's surfing as "stand-tall-and-do-nothin'-at-all," but the guys taking pictures for the magazines knew the art was in the subtleties and found him an attractive subject.

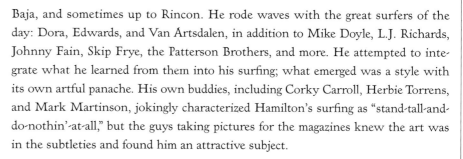

Below: Hamilton, early 1970s, a wedding guest in a cowboy shirt at Kaua'i's Valley of the Gods

Right: Hard off the bottom at Pupukea; a full-rail turn will send him straight into the guts of the wave ahead, 1971

By '63, he was a member of the prestigious Windansea Surf Club and traveled with the team to the '64 Makaha Surfing Championships, where he encountered the first big waves of his life and was plucked from the rip and, likely, from drowning by the great Hawaiian beachboy, Blue Makua. Back in the mainland, he got a job at Cabell's newly opened Charthouse restaurant in Newport Beach, and found himself right in the middle of the thriving '60s California surf scene; he got into weed, then tried LSD.

"Surfers being thrill-seekers, we were virtually taking off on a big wave." He recalls surfing under the influence: "I sat on my surfboard feeling the ocean going up through my spine and bathing my head with this warmth. I would say that if

there was a benefit from any of that, of the psychedelic era, it was that it opened our Western minds to Eastern forms of thought and belief and philosophy and a really interesting kind of thinking."

Convinced that it was the surfing life for him, Hamilton graduated from high school in June of '66 and moved straight to Hawaii. "I had been voted the fifth best surfer in the world that year in the Surfer Magazine Poll," he chuckles, shaking his head, "but that amounted to jack-shit the first time I paddled out at Sunset Beach and got my white little butt kicked all the way back to the beach." Like everyone else, he paid his dues and climbed the ladder, sharing the greatest waves in the known world (the North Shore's "Seven-Mile Miracle") with the likes of accomplished watermen (awesome swimmers, divers, and big-wave riders) like Peter Cole, José Angel, Kimo Hollinger, Ricky Grigg, Warren Harlow, Kealoha Keio, Buzzy Trent, and Tiger Espere. His peers were Jock Sutherland, Jeff Hackman, Barry Kanaiaupuni, Gerry Lopez, Reno Abellira, and "the truly great big-wave rider of our generation, Eddie Aikau."

Hamilton's life always seemed to flow along special lines of fate and serendipity. His good looks and photogenic surfing style caught the attention of Laguna Beach cinematographers Greg MacGillivray and Jim Freeman, in Hawaii shooting their surf film, *Free and Easy,* and they signed him to costar with Martinson, a hot competitive surfer from Long Beach. A pairing of opposites, the two became great friends during the filming on Oahu and then Kaua'i.

"Actually," Bill admits, "all of *Free and Easy* is me on acid. I was eatin' that stuff like candy. Greg didn't notice, but Mark . . . you could see it in the film. I was like, 'Yeah, whatever,' and Mark was like this little bulldog. He'd be drinkin' his rum and coke, and I'd be smokin' and takin' lysergic."

That was the winter of 1966–67, when Kaua'i was still relatively untouched by development. "It was like coming back into a time warp," Hamilton recalls with a grin. "There was a handful of guys that surfed out here at Hanalei regularly, but the whole time we were here, we never saw anybody." Although he lived on Oahu for another five years, the Garden Isle haunted him. "In the back of my mind, I always knew I wanted to live here on Kaua'i."

It was around this time that Hamilton met Laird and JoAnn, who were part of the MacGillivray-Freeman entourage. Laird, not yet three, was fatherless, and JoAnn was five years older than Hamilton, but there was something fate-filled about their encounter. "We all fell in love," he says. "I was nineteen years old, thinkin' it all out, makin' the decision to do this."

Hamilton and JoAnn were married in February of '67. They lived on the North Shore, right at Pipeline, for a couple of years, while he nursed a pro surfing career as a Surfboards Hawaii team rider and got a planer and took a crash course in shaping. His surfboard model was called "The Stylist." He hit the road again for MacGillivray-Freeman's next film, *Waves of Change*—which took him and Martinson on to France, Spain, Portugal, Puerto Rico, and New York City (where he met the great waterman Johnny "Tarzan" Weissmuller (1904–1984) in an elevator at *The Johnny Carson Show*). A year later, he had a key role in Severson's opus, *Pacific Vibrations*.

About then a young surfer named Bunker Spreckels was making an impression in the powerful North Shore surf with his strange little boards and committed surfing. He was living up in the hills in a World War II bunker (fittingly); he'd come down early in the morning to surf at Pipeline, then take a shower at the Hamiltons' and fall into Laird's playpen for a nap. Suddenly, this homeless surfer, who turned out to be the stepson of film actor Clark Gable, inherited the Spreckels sugar fortune and moved from the bunker to a house on Kaua'i, where he soon became bored and invited Hamilton to come over and play.

"You have to understand, I was a little kid that grew up pretty much alone on this huge beach in Laguna in the '50s, and coming to Kaua'i was like comin' back home—I loved it," Hamilton says. So he moved his family (including newborn Lyon) to relatively primitive living conditions on Kaua'i. "It was a profound experience for all of us," he readily admits. "Really, the interrelationship of being a white person here in an area where it was predominantly local . . . it was really interesting."

Hamilton is a great storyteller. His depiction of accents—especially local pidgin—is nonpareil . . . and so you tend to hang on every word.

"In the '70s, a few families controlled things out here. It was a reign of terror; of intimidation . . . rape and pillage, you name it. Now it's referred to as the 'blue truck era,' because they all drove these blue pickup trucks with chrome rims and big studded tires. It was a period known for its local hostility, and that's where Kaua'i got its bad reputation."

So one day Lyon comes home from school with a bloody nose, and Hamilton wants to know who did it, and Lyon says it had been two bigger kids, brothers in the dominant "blue truck" family. Hamilton tells Laird, who is now a big kid and has weathered plenty of his own storms in the local schools, to look into it. Laird confronts the bullies, who run to their father, "the baddest of the bad." A message comes back to Hamilton: the father wants to see him at three o'clock. He goes immediately, showing up at the guy's place before lunch. There are several sizable clan members around, and the father says, "I thought I told you three o'clock," and Hamilton says, "I don't work for you, and I don't do what you say. If you want to talk, let's talk now." The father becomes threatening, and the others crowd around him. But Hamilton shows no fear and points out that such a big, bad man shouldn't need help. So the father punches out on the time clock. "Come with me, Hamilton," he says and heads off into the woods. As soon as they're into the trees, Hamilton pulls him around. "We can take care of anything right there," he says. They square off, and the father pulls out a big knife. True to his training from brother Gordon, Hamilton peels off his T-shirt, wraps it around his hand, and says, "Okay, let's go!"

Seeing the *haole's* level of preparedness, the father reconsiders the situation and puts away the knife. "Hey, Hamilton," he says, "this should be between the kids, eh?" And Hamilton says, "Not when it's two big kids on one little kid. I don't want my boy getting beat up any more, understand?" And the father concedes. "Okay, brah. I talk wid 'em, eh?" From then on Hamilton was given a greater measure of respect and a wider berth.

Kaua'i was a tough place to eke out a living for a family of four, and periodic movie work wasn't going to do the job (at one point he did stunt work and

Hamilton worked as a surfing stunt double and helped Greg MacGillivray with the second-unit filming on the 1978 John Milius film, *Big Wednesday.* Over the years, sporadic work for such Hollywood productions helped keep the wolf away from the door.

doubled for actor Jan Michael-Vincent in John Milius's *Big Wednesday*), so Hamilton scraped together enough cash to buy a used twelve-foot boat and some gear and got into fishing . . . and into trouble.

"I left early one morning and went up past Kilauea lighthouse—about a four-mile run. I got into chasing the birds around, so I went out and out, and it was a beautiful day. I wasn't thinking, obviously, but I was new to this whole deal. Then I was gettin' kinda low on fuel, so I turned for home. I was coming into Hanalei, about two miles out, and. . . ."

He ran out of gas. No problem, he thought, and fired up the spare engine, a little Seagull. It carried a quart of gas, usually an hour's worth, but there was a strong current running, and the wind was pushing the boat sideways. He'd made very little progress by the time he ran out of gas again.

"I don't have any oars, I don't have any fins, I have nothing," he recounts. "So I jump overboard with a line attached to the boat, and I swim for three hours without stopping, and I'm further out in the ocean than when I started." By the time he crawled back into the boat, the sun was lowering toward sunset and he'd drifted down off the remote Napali coast. "Next stop's Niihau," he continues. "If I miss Niihau, I'm goin' to Tahiti. I've caught one fish—about twenty pounds—and no water. I have a T-shirt, trunks, and that's it. It's looking pretty grim, and by now I'm about five miles out."

It was too far to swim in that current. Besides, you always stay with your boat. But the sun was sinking lower. "I was getting pretty scared. Reality was setting in. I was thinkin' about Laird and Lyon and JoAnn, and how they're gonna start to get worried, and nobody knows really where I went—I didn't have a float plan. I was surveying all the things I didn't do right, and I was goin', '*Wow.*' So I just sat for a minute. I put my head down and prayed. I said, 'Jesus, you say "ask and ye shall receive," and I am asking you with all my life to help me.'"

Suddenly he realized he had a couple sticks of bamboo, used for spreading the fishing lines out from the boat so they don't get tangled. He tied his blue T-shirt onto one of them and started waving it back and forth. "I did that for about an hour, and the sun's setting . . . it's gettin' dark . . . and out of nowhere—and this is 1976, and *nobody* was out there in those days—there was a fishing boat comin' up from Napali and a sailboat, too! And they both converged on me at the same time." He laughs with revisited relief. "That was the one time when I ever really p-p-prayed for my life," he says, the stutter a clue to the intensity of the memory, "because I knew I was a dead duck."

He had a few decent years of fishing, and then a few excellent ones. Even so, JoAnn soon tired of the remote, pressurized existence and moved back to Oahu; they divorced in '77. Four years later, in an accidental meeting, he found his soul

"Mowing foam" is the surest career path for Hamilton and many of his peers. At work in his Hanalei shaping room in January of 2001

mate in Rhonda Reimers, who'd been a family friend, a baby-sitter to Laird and Lyon years earlier.

Now, Laird and Lyon were big, grown men, and Laird had become arguably the most astounding surfer on the planet, the first guy to be towed into the giant outer-reef waves of Jaws (Lyon was the fourth). This "unridden realm" became the new terrain of surfing's new millennium. In the early '90s, Laird, Buzzy Kerbox, Darrick Doerner, and Gerry Lopez began experimenting with slingshotting one another into four- and five-story waves, using tow lines behind jet skis, like water-skiers. With this "jet-assisted take-off," they could get into the swells early and with enough speed to make it down the face to ride and survive bigger waves than anything previously attempted.

"Somebody once wrote that big-wave riders are born and not made," Hamilton says. "I don't know who said it, but it's really true. It takes a certain kind of psyche to really enjoy that."

In recent years, Hamilton's spent some time with Laird and his fellow tow-in pioneers at the outer-reef spots. He's seen them ride those monster waves; he's built boards for them, and he's even done a little smaller-scale towing-in, himself. So he knows what he's talking about when he says, "They don't do it for any other reason other than that they really do love it. I've seen Laird and Darrick go out alone when it's *humungo,* and they don't care. They're going to these phantom places that you can't even see; there's nobody to watch them. They're doing it for their own love of it; they push the envelope, and they push the adrenaline button. They like the high they're gettin' from doin' that. It's an extreme place to be, and they have tempered themselves to face these big, destructive forces, to ride on top of 'em and be comfortable with 'em, and it's really become their own personal sport. They have that spirit—that gladiator spirit."

I mention the parallels between his stepbrother, Gordon, and Laird, how they both had that warrior's psyche.

"I find the whole symmetry of the entire connection, the parallels, are absolutely mind-boggling," Hamilton admits. "Just the fact that I had a father who was a stepfather who had a son, Gordon, who was my half-brother, who was really a lot like Laird, who is my stepson and stepbrother to my son. It's all so fascinating to me." He pauses, considers, then continues.

"My father did a lousy job with my brother; he was an abusive stepfather. To me it was so unfair, it really was. So when I became Laird's father, if anything, I became the opposite of my father by making Laird's life more . . . I was disciplined with Laird, and I was stern with Laird, but I was never cruel to Laird, and I was never jealous. I think that was one of the reasons I was so willing to take on Laird at a young age—because of that injustice that I saw—in some unknown depth of me."

THE DEEP-THROATED SOUNDS OF THE JET BOAT'S twin engines rumble up from the river. There's a good hour to go before sunset, an hour and a half till it's dark. Hamilton is standing in Laird's sixteen-foot-long, camouflaged Yamaha Exciter, the one he uses to tow-in at the island's other outer-reef spots. The five seats are made of inflated rubber, and there are handholds in a few strategic places, but none for the passenger in the middle-rear, which is where I sit, next to the driver's seat. It's my last night on the island, and Hamilton's taking me for a spin. "Hey son, can I borrow the keys to the car?" he jokes.

Laird keeps the boat and his camouflaged jet ski a hundred yards upstream, in a small cul-de-sac below the land he recently purchased. He's been clearing away the hau and mango for a house. In the meantime, when he's off island, well . . .

As we tool slowly down the green river, it feels like we're somewhere in Southeast Asia. Hamilton's voice is low as he talks about Laird and surfing and his life as a series of miracles. "History repeats itself. The cycles always kind of glance off each other as they come around full circle. It's like the longboard thing, which we thought was a lost art. Then it came back in and rejuvenated the surfboard industry, brought back a lot of our roots and our history. Every generation should be aware of the great lineage that we travel in. I mean, we're surfers, y'know? I'm proud to be a surfer. I've been a student of the game for so long, and, in a real pure sense, I *love* to surf. And I love everything that surfing has done for my life, in the sense of where I live. I mean, look at this place where I live. This is a beautiful environment, and I'm here because I love to surf. I'm one of the rare people in the world that gets to do something that they love for work, and when I'm in the water I see it put a smile on somebody's face. That's a gift, it really is."

The jet boat clears the river mouth and Hamilton taxis it slowly out along the reef at Hanalei until we're well out beyond the pier and beyond the boats anchored nearer shore. Then he throws back the throttle and blasts across the bay like a maniac, heading toward Lumahai at the opposite end of the big bay. When we get there, he strafes the beach, expertly whips the thing into a 180, then vaults back across the bay, leaping the boat from swell to swell until we reach a nondescript patch of water about a mile off the point at Princeville.

He eases off the throttle and trolls around. "This is where we were riding the boat last Memorial Day," he says. "That was something! It's about sixty feet deep here; the waves had 100-foot faces. Whew!"

Today, it's only a foot or two, but as he turns back towards Hanalei, one of the engines goes completely dead, and the other begins to sputter. Soon we are making only intermittent progress—less than a mile an hour—and I start to measure the swim I seem about to make. I can't help but notice the sun is setting.

"Good thing it's not as big as it was last time I was out here," he says, flashing that big Hamilton grin. "If it was, we'd be dead."

Sliding into a big, clean wall of water at Waimea Bay, December 1973, Hamilton lets the speed build before he commits to a series of stylish maneuvers.

The site of the first major surfing contest of the post–World War II era, Makaha Beach has it all—playful surf when it's small like this, and some of the biggest, most dangerous waves in the world when it's huge.

an (male and female) is a territorial and competitive creature. Thus, as surfing was thoroughly integrated into pre-contact Hawaiian culture, so was competition on the waves. And when surfing was resuscitated and revived in the early-twentieth century, competition, too, was swiftly resurrected.

Precise goals are difficult to establish in the dynamic near-shore wave environment (what exactly do you measure in determining surfing prowess?), so early-twentieth-century surf contests were focused on paddling races. These generally involved a "beach start," racing around a prescribed course (usually marked with one or more buoys), then crossing a finish line. Often there were multiple circuits of such a course; sometimes the contest was won by the paddler who covered the most distance in the time allocated.

Wave riding was integrated into these events in the most ancient and natural of ways: if a wave came along and accelerated your progress, that was a good thing. You could stand to ride it or you could remain prone and guide the board down the wave and toward the beach, maintaining maximum speed in the direction of the goal. If you stood, any maneuvering brought the risk of a fall and the loss of your board, which could be a serious development, so a conservative approach was most common.

It wasn't until the Makaha International Surfing Championships of the mid-1950s, held at Makaha Beach on the west side of Oahu, that subjective scoring entered the contest picture. Performance criteria included wave selection, positioning, and length of ride. So, the surfer who caught the biggest wave and rode it for the longest distance in the most critical part of the wave was theoretically awarded the greatest number of points.

All of this was very rational but somehow contrary to the emerging ethos of the psychedelic '60s, when the "artform" of surfing became a consideration. Competition, by then institutionalized and overseen by various regional, national, and global organizations, attempted to adapt to the times by including factors like style and the number and "radicalness" of the maneuvers performed in their various judging criteria.

But the spell of objectivity was weakened in those days, and surfers shifted away from the contest paradigm. The trifold impulses of drugs, draft evasion, and localized surfboard production tended to decentralize the sport and drive it into the hinterlands. The briefly presentable, cartel-dominated sport of the mid-'60s returned to the underground, where its mythological roots had been nourished throughout the previous decades and, indeed, since the missionary times.

The fading calls of vanishing pied pipers (surfers like America's Mickey Dora and John Peck, or Australia's Nat Young and Wayne Lynch, or the hundreds of others gone seeking after bluer pastures) turned most heads away from the world of prizes and trophies and toward the essential core values inherent in the act and process of riding waves.

Since the evolution of surfing is embodied in its most eloquent practitioners—those masters of the dance who embarrass all others with their grace under pressure—and these best surfers were drifting away from the heat of organized battle, the sport drifted rather aimlessly into the '70s.

Rolf Aurness

Stairway to Heaven

THE TRANSFORMATION OF ROLF AURNESS

Rolf Aurness grabs his board, prepared to launch into action at the Banzai Pipeline, December 1969

In May of 1970, a tall, lean eighteen-year-old California goofy-foot named Rolf Aurness became the world surfing champion by overwhelming a stellar group of finalists— including Midget Farrelly, Peter Drouyn, Reno Abellira, Keone Downing, and Nat Young—surfing almost exclusively backside in a decidedly low-key competition held at a remote southern Australia beach. Despite the obscurity of the venue, Aurness' victory rallied considerable media coverage, largely because he was the son of the famous actor James Arness, who played Marshall Matt Dillon in the long-running *Gunsmoke* television show, which was nearly as popular in Australia as it was in the United States. "Marshall's Son Wins World Surf Shootout" was a typical Aussie headline.

The rise of Aurness from obscurity to the world title was classically meteoric. But after winning his world title, Aurness seemed to fade from the scene even faster than he'd arrived, although with less media coverage. Those were twilight years for surfing and American society in general; the pot had been stirred by the turbulence of the '60s, and the new paradigm had not yet jelled. When the final world contest was held in San Diego in '72, Aurness was not there to defend his title, but neither were any other former champions, so it seemed almost natural—as if it was mostly a comment on the state of competitive surfing. And by the time the pro tour kicked into gear in '76, the twenty-four-year-old former world champion was like the distant ghost of a bygone era—nowhere to be found and on nobody's mind.

The truth of Aurness's rise and fall is more accurately portrayed as an orbit or an arc—one that had deep roots in the invisible, burst above the horizon for a brief and spectacular time, then set once again in the West. But just as the sun doesn't die at the end of each day, neither did Aurness really disappear. He was just going through his changes, journeying on the dark side, heading for the next new dawning.

ON AN EARLY AFTERNOON IN OCTOBER OF 2000, in the highly congested and renovation-rich zone known as Brentwood Village, just west of the San Diego freeway in Santa Monica, I find Aurness at the corner Starbucks—a long, lean guy slouching beneath a baseball cap at an outside table. The logo on the cap reads, "Butt Juice Surfboards."

The morning after he won the 1970 world contest, Aurness took his dog for a run on the low-tide sand at Torquay in Australia.

His chiseled face is more like his dad's than I remembered, but the familiar high-pitched laugh is as young as ever. We walk down the street to a sprawling stucco apartment complex, where he's lived for the last eight years or so. His dad lives a few blocks away; they check the surf together on Tuesday and Thursday mornings.

Aurness's apartment isn't as messy as he made it sound on the phone, but it's dim and drab and, yes, a little messy. Lying on the ocher shag carpet is a sweet blue surfboard with a Butt Juice logo. He shows me the other room and his Frank Zappa album collection. We sit at the table and talk, catch up on things. He brews us cups of an Amazon tea—green, tannic—a "combo of herbs from the jungle" prescribed for his liver.

As we're talking, his girlfriend Chenoa calls. She grows plumeria in Malibu and has called with Aurness's reading for the day: "I pray that I may let God's spirit come into my heart. I pray that it may fill me with an abiding peace." Then she adds, "Relax." He calls her Chen (pronounced *Shen*), and they've been together for almost twenty years. They have a lot in common. "I don't know if she's really my girlfriend," he jokes, but he could be serious.

After a while, Aurness asks me if I'd like to go down the block to the soup shop. "It's homemade," he encourages, and we do. The neon sign on the window proclaims *Organic*. Inside, a savvy young boy waits on us, brings soups as thick as porridge, makes Aurness' smoothie just the way he likes it.

Aurness tells me he's got high cholesterol, so he's on a special diet. He eats chicken, fish, turkey, and those organic soups and smoothies. He has a theory that the excessive cholesterol might be produced by a liver stressed from years of surfing the chilly Hollister Ranch area ("The Ranch" is about twenty-five miles west of Santa Barbara) in severe conditions. Besides the diet, which includes carrot juice and wheat grass, he tries to walk two miles every day.

"How often do you surf?" I ask.

He laughs. "Oh! . . . ha-ha! . . . well . . . I make my annual trek to San Onofre!" He says his father went with him in August this year. The surf was up, and he confides with an unabashed laugh, it was a struggle to make it out through the breaking waves.

The next morning, we're scheduled to have a late breakfast with his father. I arrive a little early and find the house—comfortable, not at all grandiose—on the south side of Sunset Boulevard. When James Arness opens the door, it takes a couple of seconds for me to adjust. The last time I remember seeing him was on the beach at Malibu looking the confident Giant Marshall in the summer of '69. Thirty years later, he's bent to my height with arthritis, his shock of light brown hair gone white. But the big grin and the penetrating eyes are unchanged.

Jim and I sit in the living room. His wife of twenty-two years, Janet, brings us tea. After a while, Rolf joins us.

The monster storm surf of December '69 tested many a surfer's mettle on the North Shore. Aurness looking ready to go at Sunset Beach in December

James Aurness was born in Minneapolis, the grandson of Norwegian immigrants. An aspiring actor, he was wounded in World War II, moved west after the war, and became one of the beach bums, living off federal disability, fishing and surfing, and drifting up to Los Angeles every so often to act in a play or to audition. By the time he married actress Virginia Chapman in 1949, he was getting movie work, including a couple of jobs in Hawaii.

Rolf was born in February of '52. *Gunsmoke* premiered in the fall of '55 and ran for twenty years, in the process transforming James "Arness" into an American icon. The work was in Los Angeles, but when it came time to get away, Jim knew where to go. He found a nice place to rent, right on the beach, with a view straight into the barrel of Makaha's famous point surf. "Those years at Makaha were a precious part of our life," he smiles and sighs. "This was the old Hawaii—a special place."

Jim developed a special relationship with the local Hawaiians; he loved to cook for them and sit around and drink and "talk story." Makaha was a sanctuary, but home was in Pacific Palisades, where Rolf went to Canyon Charter School and

Opposite: "What are you going to do with your life? What's your goal?" Aurness at Waimea, December 1969

showed an early interest in boxing, much to the chagrin of his mother, who didn't like him hanging around with his surf pals, either. It wasn't until the summer of his high-profile divorce ('60) that Jim finally hauled Rolf down to San Onofre to introduce him to his friends and his secret love, the ocean. When Rolf graduated from an air mattress to an eight-foot surfboard, Jim entered him in the boys division of a San Onofre contest, and he won. He was stoked on surfing.

Then, in '61, Rolf fell out of the backyard treehouse and smashed his head on the stone slab below. "I think I hit almost head-first," he recalls. "I lost consciousness there for a while, but I woke up and walked up to the house, and our nanny started screaming—blood was streaming down—and she took me up to the doctor, whose name was Dr. Martini." Rolf laughs, remembering. "He was a funny guy."

Martini stitched the boy up, but Rolf could only make gurgling sounds, and lost consciousness again. At the hospital, it was discovered that his skull was punched open, and three shards of bone protruded into his brain. "They operated

right away, but we didn't know what to expect for forty-eight hours," Jim recalls. "When he woke up, the doctor asked him some questions about the accident, and he talked normally. Boy, were we ever relieved!"

Seeing your child suffer such a debilitating, near-fatal injury can affect a parent in different ways. For Virginia, it was time to put on the brakes, but Jim felt it was imperative that young Rolf work through it. "I really pushed him," he admits. "When this happened, it was devastating because I hated thinking of him not being able to surf."

Jim held firm, insisting on nothing less than full-bore rehabilitation. He developed a training program and devoted himself to Rolf's recovery. "He had a hole in his skull with nothing but skin covering the brain, and that took a long time to fill in, so we got a baseball batter's helmet, and I sawed off the bill." He duct-taped it to Rolf's head for surfing.

"We'd get up at dawn and go down there every morning," Jim says. "He'd surf with the businessmen who were out before work. Every day, whether it was eight feet or eight inches." Terrified that Rolf might "think of himself as a cripple," Jim took the boy to every contest on the coast. "He kept charging and winning, right through each division. We had a great time through those years."

"Dad became my mentor and coach," Rolf says. "He entered me in contests, took me up and down the coast to compete, took the motorhome to Baja. I concentrated only on surfing for the next ten years—San Onofre all summer, Makaha and the North Shore three times a year, Hollister Ranch, plus I practiced in Santa Monica before and after school."

Jim's pride in his son's recovery and achievements belied deeper motives. "Dad was a huge Hollywood personality," says Rolf. "But he felt that his own success was almost totally due to luck or some kind of divine providence. He had seen hundreds of people in the business who never made it, who had horrible lives, and he didn't want that to happen to us."

Quiet and unassuming though he was, Rolf blazed a trail through the South Coast boys' circuit, moved into the juniors with his friends Brad McCaul and

Corky Carroll, and won there, too. He became a team rider for Bing Surfboards and—just sixteen—shocked the elite ranks of the newly created AAAA circuit by earning a spot on the West Coast team at the '68 world contest in Puerto Rico. He dominated the circuit again in '69, unseating Carroll from his longstanding spot atop the Western Surfing Association ratings and earning the first position on the U.S. mainland team for the '70 world contest in Australia.

With such success, Rolf seemed to emerge from his father's shadow. In Hawaii for the arrival of the historic big winter swells of '69, he was one of a

handful of big-wave riders who paddled out to ride the giant Makaha surf on the morning of December 4th, the milestone day that tombstoned Greg Noll's great surfing career.

"After that experience at Makaha, I got this feeling that I was getting close to achieving my goal of actually challenging nature, of putting my manhood on the line," Rolf recalls. "We drove up to Waimea—Corky, Mark Martinson, and I—and it was huge, and Eddie Aikau was on the beach. 'It's closed,' he said. 'You can't go out'—because it was so big. I thought long and hard, standing there at Waimea and watching. I'd never ridden the place, and it was *mean*. But I finally said to myself, 'Well, here I am. What're you going to do with your life? What's your goal?' And I picked up my board and walked down and paddled out."

Rolf describes it as one of "life's most astounding experiences" and marks the day as the beginning of his personal transformation. "I actually had a feeling that my life was saved or protected that day, and that's been with me ever since. It was a feeling of some kind of higher power. The first wave that I rode, I dropped in and the first fifteen feet was just a freefall straight down. I actually felt it was like a near-death or out-of-body experience. I almost felt a kind of light—a kind of a message in a way—and I finally made it to the bottom and made the turn. After that I said, enough is enough. I think this is what led me, after the world contest, to say, well, I don't really have to pursue those goals any longer."

Among his peers, Rolf was the most popular surfing champion ever. Not only was he a great surfer, he was energized, self-effacing, humble, good-looking, and apparently optimistic. Apparently, because an external struggle for control between his mother and father was reflected in an internal struggle for understanding and direction.

In the late '60s, his mother's Malibu Canyon house became a wild cultural stew—celebrities, hippies, gays and lesbians, musicians, drug dealers, you name it. "The parties became a lifestyle for many people," Rolf says. "It can take a hold of your life."

His sister Jenny wanted Rolf to be more socially active, to put the surfing life (and his famous father) behind him. During the summer of '70, the siblings rented a cottage in Topanga Canyon (about thirty miles west of Hollywood). One evening, Rolf went out to walk the fire trails and watch the sun set and met a young man who turned out to be a "psychedelic guru." He gave Rolf a hit of LSD, and later that night Rolf had a vision of Jacob's ladder—like a dream, but exceptionally powerful. "I realized there were gonna be some serious repercussions from the experience," he admits, "because a lot of people don't know how to handle that."

In this vulnerable state, Jenny introduced Rolf to an older woman named Kiyo, an "astrologer to the stars," who began to guide him toward a reevaluation of himself and his destiny in life. But Rolf—disturbed by his parents' conflict, let down after his surfing success, confused by fame, and split open by LSD—was spiraling out of control. "I think growing up becomes a personal battle," he says. "For me it was a matter of humility—realizing that we're not rock stars, that we can't lead that lifestyle."

Rolf entered a psychiatric unit in '72 and didn't make the world contest that year. The following summer, he and Kiyo were married. "She said that through practice you can get high without the LSD, and she started taking me down to the Philosophical Research Society in Hollywood," he explains. "There was a little

Looking like a cross between his father and Clint Eastwood, Aurness contemplates the distant horizon from the beach in Australia, 1970

psychedelic influence in there, too, but I think the experiences that I had through my wife kind of became my lifestyle."

As his surfing life faded, he took up jazz piano, essentially following his own path. "I became interested in the pure art of improvisation, but it was a double-edged sword because I never pursued technical lessons and never learned—it was over quick," he admits. "But, for the record, all the jazz led me into Zappa."

Then, in '75, his sister (who was dating Greg Allman of the Allman Brothers Band at the time) died of a heroin overdose; within a year, his mother ended her life, too, and in '78, cancer had taken Kiyo. In less than four years, the three key people in his life—the three women—were taken.

A few years earlier, Jim had finished construction on his house and barn up at the remote Hollister Ranch. Rolf and Kiyo drove up there every so often, and Rolf was getting into the water again, testing a new "hydroplane" surfboard design. The wind-swept slopes and solitude provided a much-needed haven from old influences that threatened to pull him back into the world of abuse. "I started surfing more, but I still liked to go to bars, so I had an inkling that I wasn't quite over all that partying yet. After my wife died and I moved to Malibu, I started hanging out with Chenoa. She was instrumental in helping me get over my wife's death.

"I was caretaker and gardener around there for those years. We studied French intensive gardening, made the raised beds, and went up and got sand and had a compost pile. Of course, the fresh vegetables . . . they taste so much better than you can get in the store."

Visitors were uncommon, but not rare. Nat Young came by with Mickey Dora in tow. Ranch regular George Greenough got Rolf interested in windsurfing, and he adapted his hydroplane theory to a sailboard. Life at the Ranch was good . . . until the place was sold in '86, shortly after Jim surfed his last wave there.

IT'S LATE IN THE AFTERNOON, and we're back in Rolf's apartment, and he's telling me about "butt juice," a phrase he uses to describe the astral light he first saw that day at Waimea Bay.

"I'm no expert," he says, "but I do seem to have some affinity or feeling towards this astral light. Several religions discuss it; Yogananda talks about it in his *Autobiography of a Yogi,* and it's mentioned in the Bible. It's the same type of feeling I had out surfing at the Ranch, and so I think it's prevalent in my life. It might even be related to the gift Kiyo tried to pass on to me through metaphysics. Y'know, we thought of the term 'butt juice' just for fun, but in a way it does have meaning. Surfing is really what provided this intuitive feeling for a higher power for me in the later stages of my life, and it's led me right into meditation."

Rolf and father Jim Arness, checkin' the surf together in 2001

Today, inspired by the teachings of the Self-Realization Fellowship, Rolf practices something called kriya yoga. "You don't have to do the postures—you can sit in a chair—but you try to look inward and clear your mind."

He works a few days a week as a volunteer at a mental-health clinic on Second Street in Santa Monica. This particular clinic offers its clients a "dual-diagnosis recovery plan," and Rolf is a kind of counselor there. "It's open every day," he tells me. "You can just come and go as you want, sit in on the groups. But my purpose there is to help the people with psychiatric disorders. If I want to hire on as a therapist at the clinic some day, I could. But there's nothing really attractive to me about monetary success."

I ask him if he thinks he'll get back into surfing again?

"Well, that's a possibility," he answers. "I think the yogis 4,000 years ago felt some of the same feelings that we feel out surfing—where you're communing with nature, and you begin to feel a higher power. Through meditation and quiet time and time in the chapel, it feels like it's almost a continuation of my surfing experiences at the Ranch. Plus, at this stage of my life . . . I'm forty-eight, and I can't perform like I used to, so it's a whole different program. That's why I like to go to San Onofre with the other old-timers."

Not that he looks that old. In fact, it's not at all hard for me to imagine Rolf picking up that blue stick and ripping apart a wave like before. I ask him to sum up his daily philosophy of living. "I'm glad to be here living my life," he tells me. "Regarding the astral worlds, I don't think about it too much. We'll be there soon enough."

We talk for a while more, then I check out the blue surfboard—the hydroplane with the Butt Juice logo. We bring it outside, to the walled-in courtyard among tiers of stucco apartments, and I take some pictures.

"You wanna go for a bowl of soup today?" he asks me after a while.

"Oh, y'know," I say, "that was pretty good."

"Yeah, it's homemade."

Aurness at the local soup and juice bar, January 2001

Ventura curl. Everything comes in waves, but these are the kind you can play with.

Zen Mind

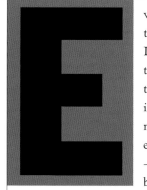**E**verything is waves. This was the vision of Albert Einstein. It is the lesson and the truth that emerges, over time, out of the surfing experience. Surfing is a natural act, but a *complex* natural act. To ride a wave is to explore the universe of balance —balance within balance within balance. Without balance, a ride cannot be sustained. Without balance, a wave cannot be sustained. Without balance, nothing can be sustained. It sounds like the ancient wisdom of Lao-tzu in the *Tao Te Ching:*

> Man's laws should follow natural laws,
> just as nature gives rise to physical laws,
> whilst following from universal law,
> which follows the Tao.

Another oft-quoted Chinese sage spoke to the subject: "Balance is the perfect state of still water. Let that be our model. It remains quiet within and is not disturbed on the surface." This is from Confucius, but as surfers we need to bend his words. Confucius was speaking to the ideal balance of the sage in meditation. But for our purposes, we can find the applicable principle within:

> Dynamic balance is the perfect state of the surfer.
> Let that be our model. To remain quiet within
> as the advancing water lifts and curls and folds
> us in the transient hollows of its surface.

At the onset of the present era, the balancing act of the surfer was obvious and celebrated. The beachboy paddled furiously to gain momentum against the uplifting wind and then, feeling at last the downward grip of gravity on his redwood plank, he rose to some statuesque position on the board, torquing ever so slightly into a lateral slide, and raising his arms to announce his successful completion of the balancing act, holding the pose for as long as the wave and his good luck allowed.

The art of precarious balancing hit its apex with the hollow boards. Those thick, lightweight, narrow-sterned, box-sided inventions were especially cumbersome and tippy and were steered at the rear from a high center of gravity. In truth, they were suited only for the rolling swell and the crumbling wave, or for the intended purpose of their inventor: efficient paddling.

It was only with the advent of the Malibu surfboards of the 1950s that stability and easy maneuverability became the focus of surfboard design. From then on, surfing moved steadily forward as a vehicle for expression and exploration, allowing surfers to ride evermore challenging waves with ever-more casual grace.

For the surfer, whose achievement is ultimately a function of poise and balance in the very midst of explosive turmoil, the *Tao Te Ching* is especially instructive:

> The natural way is the way of the sage,
> serving as his dwelling,
> providing his centre deep within,
> whether in his home or journeying.
>
> Even when he travels far,
> he is not separate
> from his own true nature.
> Maintaining awareness of natural beauty,
> he still does not forget his purpose.
>
> Although he may dwell in a grand estate,
> simplicity remains his guide,
> for he is full aware, that losing it,
> his roots as well would disappear.
> So he is not restless,
> lest he loses the natural way.

Gerry Lopez

Cakewalk

GERRY LOPEZ, THE BUDDHA IN THE BARREL

The jet stream had bulged low over the Pacific, moving the storm track way down close to the Hawaiian Islands, then sweeping back to the northwest, heading straight across California. While Seattle was uncharacteristically dry for late December, Los Angeles was drowning and the mountains—from San Diego to Oregon—were getting major dumps. ❧ In the midst of these meteorological aberrations, Gerry Lopez, the genie of consummate positioning, had once again found the perfect spot to take off. Poised in the near-vertical lip of the arcing cornice, he looked left, then right; he was alone in the lineup. He looked straight down the clean, virgin slope, took a deep breath, and

Gerry Lopez, dripping with saltwater, post-session, 1997

(without a stroke) dropped down the huge wall. His board gathered speed quickly; he could feel the energy building in his legs and feet. He continued to drop, letting it build, and build, and then (sensing some g-force red-line and imminent meltdown) he set his board on edge and carved one wicked, deep, delicious, stoking bottom turn. Then: cutback, bottom turn, cutback, bottom turn, cutback, bottom turn, cutback, bottom turn, and on and on. And all the while the huge white wave stood tall and patient and wide open. It was the ride of the day on Mount Shasta, and by the time he pulled out at the bottom new snow had filled his tracks at the top.

"Bitchin'!" said Lopez.

IF YOU'RE A SURFER, HIS NAME MIGHT RING A BELL: Gerry Lopez. Frolicking with the other school kids in the waves at Honolulu's Ala Moana harbor entrance in the late '60s. Boring through big Pipeline barrels in the early '70s. Immortalizing the lightning bolt and pathfinding in Bali in the mid '70s. Lighting up Java and Grajagan in the late '70s. Windsurfing the north shore of Maui in the '80s, and towing into monster Jaws peaks in the '90s.

I spent many hours on the beach in front of Lopez's North Shore home while he was the reigning Mr. Pipeline, a title that had passed to him from Butch Van Artsdalen. In fact, I sat next to Van Artsdalen, both of us watching Lopez enveloped in his peculiar aura of mastery, owning that near-mythic wave like no one else—not Butch or Phil Edwards (who rode the first recorded wave there) or John Peck or Jock Sutherland—had ever owned it. Never had a surfer defined a particular spot like Lopez defined the so-called Banzai Pipeline, and never had a particular wave so defined a surfer.

Because of this (and succeeding actions) Lopez became a cultural icon—a definitive archetype of what being a surfer is all about. He is master of the game. Surfing or life. In a way, he might say, it's all the same. Surfer, shaper, biker, cinema sidekick, sage, splatball warrior, traveler, husband, father. . . . It's a question of balance—of what balance means and of what balance can achieve. Because somehow, now at age fifty-four, Lopez continues to extend the unique envelope of his life in new directions, all the while maintaining a solid connection with the planet's most esoteric regenerative medium—the barrels of excellent waves.

I visited Lopez in '91, wound up the road from Makawao to his twenty-acre homestead on the slopes of Haleakalā Crater, not far from where Woody Brown had his own divine revelation. Down there, the north shore beaches of Maui were distant and muted—a panoramic meditation in pastels. On a big winter's day, swells rippled toward shore in achingly slow motion. Whitewater formations—surreally suspended—blossomed in silence far below. Up there in Olinda, where he lived with his wife, Toni, there was only the rush and rattle of monster eucalypti, the hiss of

Master of the medium, relaxed in the fierce fold of a Pipeline curl, Lopez's sheer consciousness of the moment seems to ensure the wave's cooperation. Late afternoon slide, c. 1980

blowing grass, and the hard, foul crackle of Lopez's somehow medieval Yamaha 125 as he kicked it to life to take his then two-year-old son Alex out for a spin.

The Lopez compound consisted of the tasty but modest home Gerry designed and built himself, his board-building shop, his brother Victor's house, and lots of grass and trees. Lopez grew protea shrubs up here in the '70s, but now he was just shaping surfboards, mowing foam with a planer or (for Styrofoam) cutting it with a hot-wire. One afternoon, he patiently answered my questions in the hush of his living room, oddly distant from the pounding waves of Pipeline and the North Shore.

He was born Gerald Ken Lopez in November of 1948. He might well describe himself as a mongrel. His father (Gerald Victor Lopez) was a Honolulu newsman, a journalist for the *Bulletin* after World War II, then twenty-five years more with the *Advertiser*. Lopez's father's father was born in Cuba; his father's grandfather was from the Canary Islands. His father's mother was born in

A perfectly timed bottom turn sets up an immaculate tube ride. Lopez plots his soulful course at Pipeline, December 1977

Germany. Lopez's mother, Fumi, was Japanese, born on Kaua'i. Lopez has an older sister, Lola, and two younger brothers, Victor and Kip, both of whom surf.

Like every South Shore kid, Lopez learned to surf in the gentle rollers of Waikiki. He attended the academically prestigious Punahou school, where Fred Van Dyke was his eighth-grade science teacher, Peter Cole was his ninth-grade algebra teacher (and "a very influential person in my life"), and Jeff Hakman was a Punahou student when he won the first Duke Kahanamoku Invitational contest in big waves at Sunset Beach in '65. "I was a senior, and he was a junior," recalls Lopez. "That was pretty far out."

Lopez honed his surfing skills at Ala Moana, the Waikiki reef that was made perfect for surfing by construction of the harbor channel and breakwall. It was the place where surfers first consciously tried to ride inside the wave. "The first time that I saw Sammy Lee and Conrad Canha get in the tube—disappear and come back out—we didn't even know what to call it," Lopez laughs. "But they were getting totally barreled back when I was still in high school. It was really bitchin'."

"Ala-Mo" was where all the good surfers came to ride the summertime south swells—Donald Takayama, David Nuuhiwa, Fred Hemmings, Van Dyke, Cole, and especially Paul Strauch, whom Lopez considered his greatest inspiration.

Lopez went on to college (a year in California, a couple of ragged years at the University of Hawaii), but he could see the pattern: "I was falling deeper and deeper into surfing." He had aimed to become an architect, but he never graduated. "I took a degree in surfing on the North Shore."

Like other kids of the era, he surfed on boards that were nine to ten feet long. The most revered shaper of the time was Dick Brewer, but he was in such high demand that it was almost impossible to get a board from him.

"I think it was late 1967. Brewer had just moved over to Maui from the North Shore and was shaping in Lahaina. Reno [Abellira] and I each took a [foam] blank over there to get our boards made by him. Reno got his shaped first, but before he could shape mine Nat Young, George Greenough, Bob McTavish, and a couple of other Aussies showed up with their short wide-tailed vee-bottom boards. John Thurston had a surf shop where all the boards got glassed, and we met 'em there, and Brewer and McTavish kind of bullshitted for a long time. So the next day we go back to do my board (I think I wanted like a 9'8", which was considered a shorter board then), and Brewer just takes the saw and cuts two feet off the blank, and it's 8'6", and he tells me, 'That's how big a board you're getting.'"

That was the beginning of the shortboard revolution in Hawaii. In another six months, another foot was lopped off and surfboard design went off in all different directions. Lopez went on to mature as a surfer in an era of free-thinking, wide-open expression, delivering radical maneuvers in an effortless style that charmed

slack-jawed peers like Jimmy Blears (who won the world title in '72), Jock Sutherland, Abellira, Jack Gonzalez, and Buddy Boy Keohe.

Although Brewer later claimed Lopez as his best shaping student, Lopez named Chris Green, a Greg Noll–trained shaper for Fred Schwartz at Surfline in Honolulu, as his primary influence (such genealogies and concomitant pedigrees are of importance to discriminating surfers). Green guided Lopez and his friend Buddy Dunphy through the process of making a board like the one Brewer had shaped. After that they made another, and then another. "Pretty soon we were doing one a week because that's how fast the boards were changing," Lopez recalls. "Chris was the guy that showed me and Dunphy the fundamentals of shaping, and then Buddy and I started building boards together."

It was about the same time that Lopez, Abellira, Keohe, and plenty of other surfers discovered yoga, meditation, and psychotropic substances, and it was on the North Shore in the winter of 1968–69 that Lopez began to generate some media buzz, making his debut in *Surfer* magazine. At the '69 Huntington Beach championships held at Huntington Pier, his innovative touches—pre-heat meditation, sideslipping as he headed toward the pilings, and that elegant flowing style—made him the unofficial winner.

Left: The dancer and the dance—off-the-lip elegance on a small day at Pipeline, c. 1980

Above: Late-breaking commitment in his third decade of mastery at Pipeline, December 1985

Right: In this game of precision timing, nature ultimately deals the cards. Lopez heads back to the shaping room after being trumped by the joker, December 1977

By the great winter of 1969–70, Lopez was fast on the way to becoming the main man at the Pipeline. With an uncanny sense of timing, definitive judgment, and 101 yards of guts, he was the standout favorite photo subject of the three great surf photographers of the era—Art Brewer, Steve Wilkings, and Jeff Divine. The aesthetic quality he created by the imposition of his natural talent on the essential perfection of the wave yielded images that were just plain orgasmic. Lopez was personally establishing the criteria for the era of the tube ride, in the midst of which he simply smiled and shrugged.

Slightly built and lithe rather than athletically solid, Lopez wasn't the kind of surfer you'd expect to last long in big surf. "I've always been kind of . . . careful," he purrs. "Kind of like a long-tailed cat in a room full of rocking chairs. I could hold my breath a long time, and I was always a good swimmer, so I wasn't too worried about getting stuck in rips, and I kind of figured out that you don't panic and swim for the channel, you stay right in it—try and go over the falls and get washed in. José Angel taught us that."

Another notable quality Lopez possessed was his attitude of respect—respect for Angel and the other great waterman pioneers of the North Shore, for instance. Through his acknowledgment of their achievements ("There was nobody there to show them the way"), he was able to reach back and connect and become "a pure source." That phrase would soon find resonance as Lopez and Surfline salesman Jack Shipley launched their own surfboard business in the summer of '71. They called it Lightning Bolt.

"It was a casual kind of deal," Lopez remembers. "There were all these underground guys building a couple boards a week in their garages, and they were doing really good work, and they needed a place to sell their boards. And then, all of a sudden, we were selling a lot of boards." Demand was so strong that Lightning Bolt was soon supporting a lot of people. It was a loose confederation of free-thinking shapers and surfers, free to experiment, come and go, consign their boards, and make a living.

Soon, under the management of Hang Ten founder Duke Boyd with Lopez as chairman of the board (all he had to do was surf and be Gerry), the Bolt Corporation became the surf-biz success story of the '70s, as it branded sportswear and licensed a broad range of products, from sunglasses to jewelry. Unfortunately, an internal power struggle tore it apart, and Lopez walked. The company was in ruins by the time the surfwear boom made millionaires out of relative upstarts in the early-'80s.

"We fucked up," Lopez summarizes. "None of us knew each other well enough to work through this period of transition or we'd all be really a lot better off, but we fucked up."

In '73, following a contest in Australia, photographer Jack McCoy took Lopez and Jeff Hakman ("kickin' and screamin,'" says Lopez) on a trip to Bali, where they were blown away by the speed, quality, and ride length of the pristine waves. The spot they surfed, Uluwatu, opened Lopez's eyes to a world of waves and exotic cultures.

"That first year the surf was like nothing you've ever seen; you couldn't imagine surf being more consistent and more perfect; just non-stop. It was me and Hakman at Uluwatu, for days on end, just by ourselves." Only a few surfers before them had ridden the far-removed spot, and things there were a little primitive. They carried their boards and gear in—a considerable trek—and then had to crawl back up the cliff at day's end, though Lopez (always in training in those days) often preferred to jog out.

The problem was that packs of monkeys would get into their gear, so they started paying village kids to carry their boards and watch the stuff. "That's kind of how that whole thing started," Lopez reflects. "Shit, if you go out there now, they've got everything—you can spend the night, they'll fix your board for you, they'll sell you boards, they've got surf shops, they've got everything right there at Uluwatu. I've never seen anything change so quick."

Lopez established a dream routine. He moved to Maui in '73 and opened a Lightning Bolt shop in Kahului. As Bali developed as a surf destination, he started to spend more time at "G-land" in Java, the next great discovery. The autumn Indonesian trips evolved into intensive training camps for the North Shore winter season. He was at the peak of his game . . . but getting better.

Icons of an era: Lopez and the Lightning Bolt logo, 1973

Being a central element in virtually every sixteen millimeter surf movie made in the '70s, from *Five Summer Stories* to *Free Ride,* Lopez was already a modest film celebrity when he got a call from John Milius (author of the famous "Charlie don't surf!" guerrilla surf session in *Apocalypse Now*). A former Malibu surf *gremmie,* Milius offered Lopez a part in his new film. "We really hit it off," Lopez says. "We had a lot in common other than surfing—military history, world history, sixties music, weaponry."

Lopez loved doing films. After playing himself in *Big Wednesday,* Milius called him for a part in *Conan the Barbarian* (1980), playing Arnold Schwarzenegger's right-hand man, Subotai. He played himself again in *North Shore* (1987), then played a Dayak in Milius's *Farewell to the King* (1990), which starred Nick Nolte. "The Dayaks are natives of Borneo," Milius explained. "They're masters of the jungle, yet Gerry was more graceful than them . . . more silent. He'd climb right up a nut tree and sit on a branch—he always appears to be moving slowly, but he's really quite fast. And he learns so fast. In *Conan,* Gerry was first to learn the swordsmanship; then he taught Arnold and the others. He's amazing, really. He can run forty miles, swim wherever he has to, and I don't think even he knew how good he was on a motorcycle."

And then came the snowboard. Laird Hamilton and other friends had been in his ear about frozen waves for a long time, but Lopez always said, "I hate the

The practice of perfection puts one on a searcher's path to many discoveries. Among them for Lopez were Java's perfect G-land waves, like this one in 1992.

In the late 1990s, Lopez pulled up stakes and moved his life and business to the east side of Oregon's Cascade Mountain Range, where he rides the snow and builds surfboards near the snowboard Mecca of Bend.

snow; it's too cold." But when he and Toni visited her parents in Redding, California, in the winter of 1990–91, she persuaded him to give it a try, and he did. Then he flew to Aspen, Colorado, and took a few weeks of lessons. "I was hooked. That was that. My snowboarding career was launched." So much so that Lopez soon moved family, home, and surfboard business to Bend, Oregon, on the eastside of the Cascade mountain range.

But before that, back on Maui, Lopez was among a core group of surfers and windsurfers conquering the "unridable" waves of the outer-reef spots such as Jaws. He had emerged as the premiere builder of the highly specialized boards (complete with foot straps) used to ride these behemoths. Lopez just does everything well.

WHILE THE WORLD HAS TURNED, Lopez has kept rock steady. He's still lean and lithe and almost always wears that whimsical-sincere-ironic-Buddha-bruddah expression. And his eyes do twinkle so under that same straight, bowl-cut hair. On the beach and in the water, he's the same person. Two feet or twenty, it's still Gerry. He's still the guru.

For Lopez, surfing has always been about having fun, and his definition of "fun" seems to include the "attainable experience" of enlightenment. The North Shore, March 1984

"Surfing requires you to deal with the Here and Now more intimately than any other thing I know," he wrote me in a recent email. "Life in general tends to lead people away from the present, making them deal with the past and future (recollection and anticipation) much more than is healthy. So surfing is a spiritually uplifting endeavor, but it takes a long time before you discover that (well, for some people . . . myself), so there are a lot of dues to pay first. I guess it must just be this phase of my life cycle that brought me together with surfing and these spiritual revelations. I think you just keep getting reborn until you figure out that enlightenment is an attainable experience, and then you try to shoot for that."

So Lopez goes about his business with a sublime blend of intention and nonchalance, a highly efficient human apparatus within which a genuine soul rides and hides and looks out. His life is a book about a journey, and you'd think it was all just your basic nirvana, but who's to say?

"Life is just like surf," he told me. "It comes up, it goes down, but there's always something happening. Perhaps the greatest lesson of surfing is the gift of spontaneous reaction—flowing with it on a wave is much easier than flowing with it back on the beach. It certainly helps you move around things that seem to stop a lot of people."

The search for perfect waves has taken surfers to the far corners of the world. Photojournalist Bernie Baker recalls this moment: "Zunzal Point guard rail, ten minutes outside of La Libertad, El Salvador, June 1970, two months after my twenty-first birthday. Moments later, caught a ride north in an empty banana truck to the Guatemala border and then to Vera Cruz, with a dawn wake-up in the desert while the drivers slept. One backpack, one board, two Mayan artifacts stuffed away in my bedroll. Never found. Made it home to Carpinteria [California] six days later with a week's worth of flu in my stomach, six months after leaving home."

Sometimes the search is not a question of distance but of courage. Young "groms" gazing into the future at Third Reef, Pipeline, 1998

Central to the spirit of modern surfing is "the search." Maybe it has always been so. Having developed the rudiments of wave riding in their home islands of the South Pacific, it is within the realm of possibility that those ancient Polynesians, who ventured north and eventually encountered the Hawaiian chain, were primarily in search of better, less-crowded surf. They certainly found it in Hawaii, and perhaps that's why they stayed.

Such conjectures aside, the search continues in the mind and heart of each surfer—the search for pinwheeling waves and deserted beaches, the search for a primal engagement with the wild. Indeed, surfing as a phenomenon (as well as a philosophy), feeds a freedom born out of real, actual, day-to-day interaction with the wild.

Encounters with the wild are ever more rare in modern mechanized cultures, yet contact with the wild restores the essential human spirit. The wild is where we come from. Every meeting with it brings us more fully into our eyes and ears and lungs and fingertips. Without the wild, we are asleep in our lives.

For the surfer, the wild is the scrape of rock and shell on our cold bare feet; the chill sluice of brine down through our wetsuit; and the early-morning offshore wind numbing our cheeks, even while the rising sun blinds our vision. The wild is the approaching dark mass of an outside set, and it is the unseen but very real possibility of moving shapes in the water close around us. The wild is the ledging section of a wave sucking powerfully over a draining reef as we claw down its sheer face.

To surf is to search, to seek out and engage with the wild. This search takes surfers to the ends of the earth and back toward its beginnings. The search leads a surfer's eyes to the horizon, seeking form in the ephemeral. The search leads a surfer's body into the time zone of eternity, where the clock slows and the atmosphere hums with sprung ions. The search leads the surfer into impossible situations with improbable results. It leaves the surfer with a mouthful of the ineffable.

The surfer's search for the wild is foreign to other ways of life—an outlaw existence in which the wild becomes the sun around which everything orbits. Everything else becomes subordinate to the search and its rich rewards of surprise, desperation, and fulfillment. It is the wild that infuses surf culture and makes it such a rich world of men and women who seek daily commerce with a morphing landscape of possibilities, of possible rewards and punishments, of long efforts made for fleeting gains. Contact and intimate interaction with wild ocean waves keep surfers alive, vital, and alert. It gives them a crazy wisdom that sometimes takes them years to know they have.

At any given time, at thousands of beaches—those dynamic, untamed fringes of the planet—surfers enter the ocean in search of the wild. In this way, they grow. Their consciousness expands, one meaningless act after another.

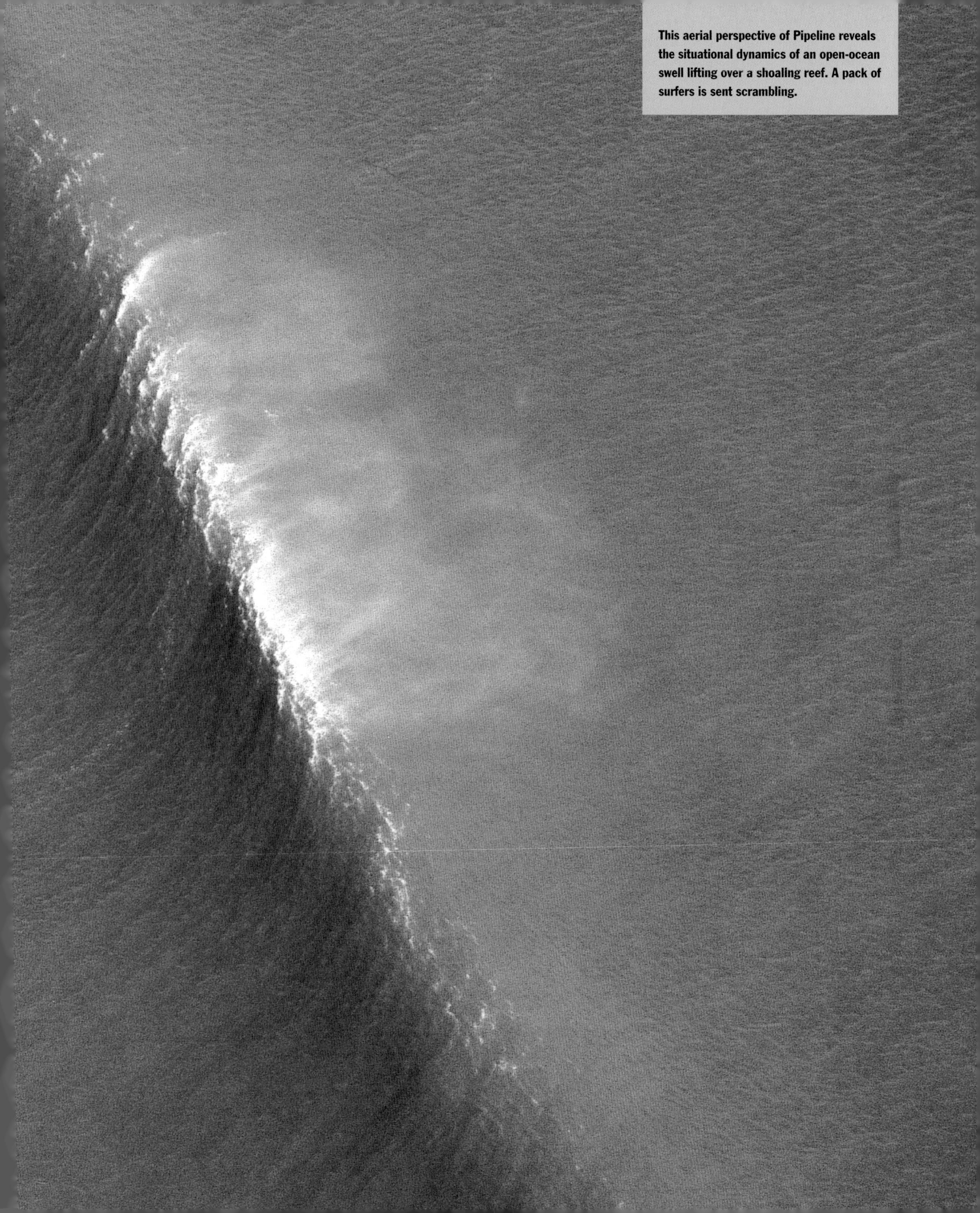

This aerial perspective of Pipeline reveals the situational dynamics of an open-ocean swell lifting over a shoaling reef. A pack of surfers is sent scrambling.

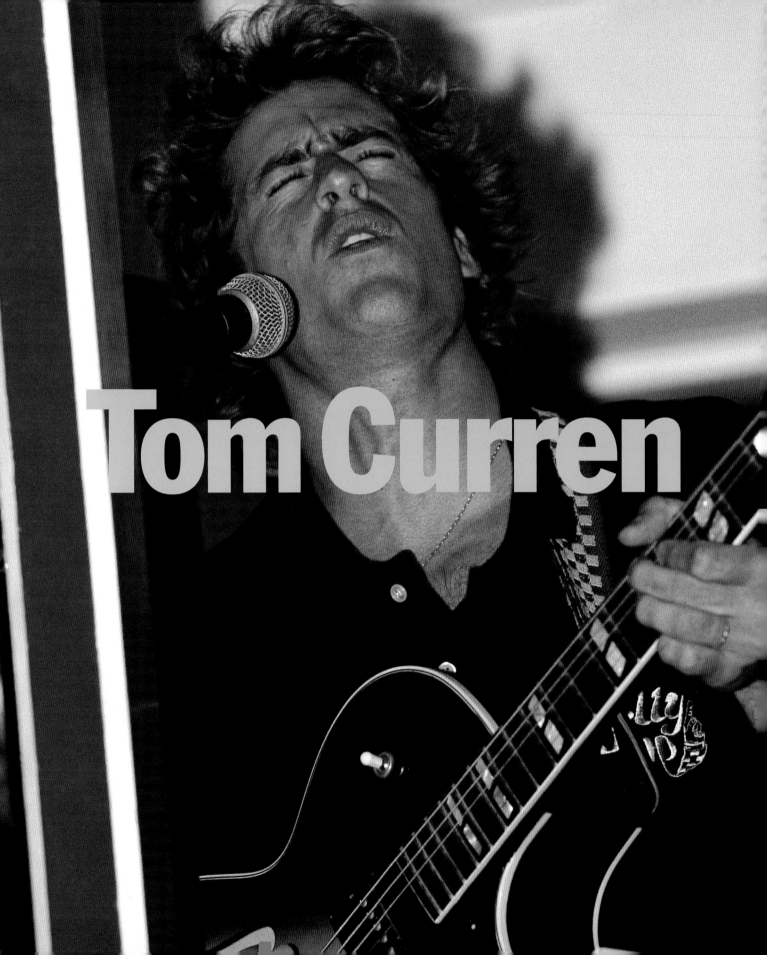

Tom Curren

The Idol

TOM CURREN, STILL WATERS RUN DEEP

Everything ends. Even in surfing, the seedbed of end-less summers, everything ends. I remember "Tommy" Curren in the autumn of 1981, shrugging off recognition while edging almost reluctantly—ah, but with such calculation—into the limelight. It seemed to me that young Curren was not going to say yes to anything but greatness. But that greatness would, of necessity, be modest because, after all, we're not great generals or artists or saviors, we're just surfers. And what does it mean to be a great surfer? Nothing at all really, but sometimes it means everything. ✺ Curren told me at the beginning: "I think He's placed me in surfing because it's my gift. It's what I do. It's what I'm gonna do. And there's a reason for that, I guess." He was

Usually the shy, silent type, Tom Curren burns down the house during a surf jam at the Kahuku Sugar Mill in December of '92

absolutely right about the gift, and that surfing was what he was going to do, and probably, too, that there was a reason for it all.

One of the great North Shore pioneers of the 1950s, Pat Curren escaped America's crowded beaches in the 1960s for the unsullied surf breaks to the south. In July of 1982, the elder Curren was in Costa Rica, surfing at Pavones and hanging with the still occasional visitor at the local cantina.

That first interview was done at his Santa Barbara, California, home, which was wedged into a narrow slice of real estate between southbound Highway 101 and its Milpas Street on-ramp. His mother, Jeanine, was a devout Christian in the truest sense of the word. On miserable nights she'd invite stranded hitchhikers inside, where they'd rest and be fed. She'd had her three kids (Tom, Joe, and Anna) with big-wave surfing legend Pat Curren one right after the other in the mid '60s. Patrick King Curren was the king of Waimea Bay back in the mid '50s, and his influence during the pioneering days on the North Shore is writ large in surf history.

"It was mostly Pat and the La Jolla guys, maybe ten guys altogether," Fred Van Dyke wrote later. "It was a three-bedroom, fully furnished place for sixty-five dollars a month across from Ke Iki Road on the North Shore. Pat went in there like always, checked it out, didn't say anything [to the landlord]. Then he lined up everybody for a meeting and the plan unfolded. Two days later, they had completely gutted the place. Just tore the insides out of it. With the leftover lumber they built surfboard racks (for their elephant guns) along the side and a giant eating table down the middle. Pat got the Meade Hall idea from the old King Arthur books. That was the meeting place for all valiant gladiators." The exploits of that "Meade Hall Gang" are pillars of surf mythology.

So the well went deep, and Tommy Curren's very cells seemed imbued with an affinity for the ocean; he reacted to it (and in it) in a way that seemed almost unconscious. Like a fish in saltwater—what waves? what ocean?

At the time, poised on the brink of a professional surfing career, the seventeen-year-old kid was somewhat conflicted in that selfsame core. "I think it's hard for them [his parents] to accept that I'm gonna be a pro surfer. Actually, my mother accepts it, but my dad's had to work all his life; he never got anything he didn't have to pay for. 'Being paid to surf?' Y'know, 'Surfing is fun! How can you do that for a living?' I'm sure he accepts it, but I'm not really sure that he understands it."

My clearest memory of that '81 visit to Santa Barbara was an afternoon go-out at the Ventura Overhead on a day so ramshackle I could make no order out of

Opposite: Nicknamed Kodak Reef by surfers in the 1970s, Off The Wall is a hollow, fast wave that's an ideal venue for great water photos of the world's best surfers. Curren, shown here in December of '87, always drew a crowd.

the shifting, funky, lopsided shorebreak. Nobody else out there—that's how junky it was—and I scarcely rode a wave. No such affliction for young Tom, who found pockets to pick, corners to cut, and plenty of holes to hide in. He took from here and there as the lackluster sea sat up and did all sorts of tricks for him—mathematically improbable in its apparent obedience to his every careless intent.

So, backpedaling, Curren started surfing at six years old with the kids of another big-wave pioneer, Buzzy Trent. This was on a visit to the west side of Oahu because, by then, Pat had met and married Jeanine and moved back to the mainland. Hawaii had already gotten too crowded for him. Thomas Roland Curren was born in Newport Beach on the eve of the '64 Fourth of July festivities. Later

in the '70s, Pat left wife and kids in Santa Barbara while he set up a life in Mexico, then Costa Rica, and, later, Mexico again.

Nonetheless inspired by his father ("He's one of the greatest men I've ever known."), Curren's talent was nurtured by a mother's love and the vision she had for him—because Jeanine knew a thing or two herself. She'd tandem surfed with the King and recognized her son's extraordinary ability to follow in the father's path, but on tiny, lightweight surfboards that resembled Pat's about as much as a stiletto resembled a broadsword.

While earning a three-point-five-plus grade-point average in his high school career, Curren honed his skills at Santa Barbara's perfect right-hand points and became world amateur junior champion in '80. He was tempted to go pro, but he wanted the men's amateur title first. That's the way Curren came out, with intent; he came on strong, but he didn't explode. A sense of pacing almost seemed his

Center: Curren digs deep, carving backside out of the pit beneath a monster wave during the 1993 Pipeline Masters strongest suit. The kid was virtually unstoppable—skinny and almost dazed with shyness, he was capable of the most flamboyant maneuvers, which were rendered almost unconsciously, but with uncanny stability.

Out of that generation of remarkable young Turks (Australia's Tom Carroll and Mark Occhilupo and South Africa's Martin Potter were contemporaries), Curren emerged as the most charismatic, the most sought-after and imitated of them all. And, like his father, the most enigmatic. He shied away. But not before racking up a couple of U.S. and amateur world titles (declining prize money along the way to maintain his amateur status), winning the first event he surfed as a pro (the '82 Marui World Surfing Pro in Japan), boycotting the apartheid-era South African leg

of the pro tour, pioneering big-wave surfing off Baja's treacherous Todos Santos Island, and winning the Association of Surfing Professionals (ASP) World Title three times, the first decided in one of the great man-on-man heats in surfing history. Curren out-duelled Occhilupo at the '86 Bells Beach Easter Classic in Victoria, Australia, emerging at twenty-one as the youngest world champion in history.

When he traveled from California to France to compete in the '80 amateur world contest, Curren fell in love with France. It was like Santa Barbara with good wine and no Santa Barbarans. On a return trip he met a beautiful local girl named Marie. They were married in '83, then he hit the road and won a few more events, including the Op Pro at Huntington Beach. After taking the Stubbies contest at Burleigh, Australia, in March of '85, Curren joined fellow pros Carroll and Potter in a boycott of South African contests. When apartheid ended in February of '91, Curren finally made the trek to that country's legendary Jeffreys Bay, where his

Right: Curren carves off the bottom at No Toes in New South Wales, Australia, in the late 1990s. This is a high-speed maneuver that the three-finned thruster surfboards helped make possible.

first wave (featuring at least three legitimate tube rides and over half a dozen monster bottom-turns/off-the-lip combos) was judged by *Surfer* magazine as one of the five greatest rides of all time.

In '86, at twenty-one, Curren became the youngest world champion of surfing ever and the first American to win the pro title. He repeated in the 1986–87 season. The most popular surfer in the world, he was featured in the July issue of *Rolling Stone* magazine, stylized as a cult hero and photographed bare-chested with his hair slicked back. After Australian Damien Hardman won the championship in '88 (an especially hard-fought contest year), Curren took a year-long sabbatical on the Cote de Basque with Marie, then decided to live in France permanently. He rejoined the pro tour in '90, winning an unprecedented seven rated events to take a third world title. In the process, he inspired fellow Santa Barbaran Kim Mearig (both rode local shaper Al Merrick's Channel Islands surfboards) to a women's world championship. He also fired the imaginations of thousands of kids and at least one Florida girl, future four-time world champion Lisa Andersen.

But things were already shifting. Largely due to the mass appeal of Curren and his peers, the ASP tour had swelled into a global circus with over two dozen rated events in a dozen countries. It was all too much; Curren abandoned the circuit after proving himself in powerful Hawaiian surf with a win in the '91 Wyland Galleries Pro. Thanks in part to a fat contract with industry giant Rip Curl, he suddenly found himself retired with a wife and two kids, a surf shop in Biarritz, France, and plenty of time on his hands to practice guitar and spearhead the Surfrider Foundation's environmental work in Europe. It seemed that not all that much distance had grown between himself and God.

His sponsorship deal with Rip Curl required only that he wear their wetsuits and clothing to work and participate in various promotions. The company adapted to their key man's shift from contest surfer to "soul surfer" with an advertising and video campaign titled "The Search." Curren would travel the world as a professional nomad, looking for perfect waves, surfing remote spots in dynamic contemplation.

"It's a marketing strategy," he laughed in '93, "but it definitely puts a different perspective on things like being a pro surfer. It gives you more of an attitude of being a tiny speck on a big planet." By then, he and Marie were in crisis, their marriage a casualty of the pro surfer's rootless lifestyle along with the added burden of living in the shadow of teen idolatry.

"Marie is a strong individual and, in certain ways, she needs to find her own creativity and her own thing," he said then. "She has a real block as far as being Mrs. Tom Curren." After attempting to establish a neutral beachhead on the Caribbean island of Martinique, the marriage dissolved and Curren began a gradual withdrawal from the public eye. Yet even as young Florida phenomenon Kelly

Curren with littoral junk, by-products of his professional edge-work on the wild stage. Ehukai Beach, North Shore, 1988

Curren usually is low-key and shy among people on land, but any hesitancy disappears as soon as he hits the water. Here, Curren charges straight into the closing hole, connecting the barrel from Backdoor Pipeline to Off The Wall, 1989

Slater burst onto the scene, winning the first of a record six world titles in '92, Curren's was an abiding mystique, and his notoriety continued to rival the new champion's. It was almost as if his sheer inscrutability, his public opacity, was a kind of reflective armor, making it easy for fans to see their projections in him.

For instance, the idea that he is a "soul surfer," a perception fed by his aversion to branding his apparel or surfboards with the customary sponsor logos: "I wouldn't really say that's an accurate description," he tells me in '03. "Surfing's my job, and I look at it that way, more than something I do to express myself or some kind of creative outlet or anything like that. Basically, I've just been surfing a long time, a lot of contests, and that kind of shapes what kind of style I have."

Shaped as it was by competition, Curren's world-famous way of surfing ocean waves—the Curren style—reads far more as innate or congenital than contest-honed. The radical fluidity of it defined an era's interpretation of the possibilities of the new lightweight three-finned aquatic vehicles, in or out of the competition context. "The reason I surf the way I do, it's just how I grew up and the principles I learned about the correct way to ride a wave."

So far, Curren has proven a rather archetypal American idol—the strong, silent type, speaking through his surfing, his music (his first CD, *Fluid,* was released in '03), and even his episodes of isolation. Now living back in Santa Barbara, father of four young surfers, married to Makeira of Panama, and once again drawing sustenance from Santa Barbara's smorgasbord of right-breaking points and plentiful reefs, he's tapping into the source of his strength. Christianity is "still my foundation," he says. "I try to stay with that basically because I had kind of gotten away from it, and I've seen where that goes."

Still waters run deep, or so it seems. Curren's stillness may be a bottomless pool of wisdom, or it could be a very real and natural modesty, a simple lack of vanity. "I was not really there for a lot of the last few years," he tells me in our most recent conversation. He is referring to the years since he left the pro tour. "It kind of isn't good just to be part of the media spin without really deserving the credit for some things. I guess I get more credit than I deserve, actually."

But he stays in the public eye, in large measure because the public won't release him. Now sponsored by The Realm, he is paid to be Tom Curren, whatever that means. He surfs a lot, he travels a little, and he appreciates it all. "I believe in God and the one creator," he says. "But at the same time, the experience we find here in this world has a lot to do with struggle and uphill, and to me that's sort of the meaning of life—work—even though people will probably laugh at that because I've got the best job you could possibly hope for."

A definitive roundhouse cutback illustrates the brilliant control and aesthetic sense of Curren, who found himself alone on this particular afternoon. "Curren's style is to show up when no one else does," said photographer Tom Servais, who also noted that the lack of logos on Curren's board dismayed his sponsors at the time.

Opposite: One of the greatest competitive surfers of all time, Curren has had a love-hate relationship with contests, sponsorship, and the media throughout his career, but his fans have always remained loyal.

The final heat of the 1964 San Clemente Surf Capades featured (left to right) contestants Joyce Hoffman, Judy Dibble, Joey Hamasaki, Linda Benson, and Margo Scotten.

New School Grrrls at Rochelle Ballard's house on the North Shore, 1994, the year Lisa Andersen won her first world title. On the deck (left to right): Ballard, Emmanuele Joli, Kim Wooldridge, Neridah Falconer, and Trudy Todd. On the steps (top to bottom): Layne Beachley, Megan Abubo, and Andersen

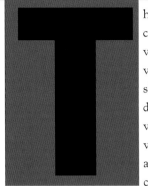

Throughout most of its twentieth-century renaissance, surfing was perceived as a man's sport, with women reduced to side-shows or accessories (as in tandem surfing). The few women who were committed to surfing were overshadowed by the astounding feats of the men, certainly in the media. Although the Makaha International Surfing Championships instituted a women's division in 1955, there were relatively few participants, and the intensity of the competition paled in comparison with the men.

Nonetheless, women played significant roles in the evolution of surfing, from ancient legend and lore (in which the wave-riding skills of Kelea and Nani equaled or surpassed that of Hawaii's most accomplished *ali'i*) to twentieth-century Hawaiian pioneers like Keanuenue Rochlen, Ethel Kukea, and Pat Honl. On the mainland, Mary Ann Hawkins and Joanne Elizabeth Trumbull preceded Gidget (Kathy Kohner) on the waves of Malibu, where women surfed in the 1950s.

The boom years of the early '60s brought a crescendo of sorts. Under the aegis of the newly formed United States Surfing Association, local, regional, and national contest systems cultivated a generation of talented young women vying for trophies and a modicum of glory. Californians Linda Benson, Phyllis O'Donnell, Joey Hamasaki, Nancy Nelson, and Joyce Hoffman and East Coaster Mimi Monroe were the shining stars in an amateur world that received polite applause from officials but was generally ignored by the ninety-eight percent of surfers who were male.

A sea change began in the late '60s, when fifteen-year-old Margo Godfrey won the world title in Puerto Rico, then went on to earn some respect for her gritty performances in the lineup at Sunset Beach and other big-wave spots. When professional surfing began to gel in the '70s, women surfers were factored in, but an attempt at parity at the '75 Lancer's World Cup in Hawaii (equal prize money was awarded to men and women) was an isolated experiment that caused a furor among the more numerous male competitors. By 1980, the men's world tour prize money had topped $225,000, while the women's purse was at an historic low—$10,000 total for the year.

Twenty years later, women's surfing was side by side with tow-in surfing as the biggest phenomena to shake up the sport since the shortboard revolution of the '60s. What made it all possible were the new "thruster" surfboards, introduced by Australian surfer Simon Anderson in 1980 and soon the world standard for high-performance equipment. Featherlight (from five to seven pounds), easy to maneuver, and fast, these three-finned surfboards leveled the playing field, reducing the medium to something akin to a skimboard—easy to carve and boost into the air, easy to duck under the waves, easy for women and girls to carry and ride.

A progression of women champions steadily raised the bar—Kim Mearig (California), Freida Zamba (four-time champion from Florida), Wendy Botha (South Africa), and Pam Burridge (Australia). Pushed virtually out of the picture by men's surfing, the new wave of young women took nothing for granted. Challenged by ever more extreme male performance standards, they pushed back, driving themselves with an urgency that soon enough began to read a lot like self-confidence. Prize money for the women, a pauper's feast at the start of the decade, grew at a faster pace than for the men and passed the quarter-million-dollar mark by '90.

After all the travel and all the contests and all the media short shrift, women's surfing finally found its galvanizing moment in the ascension of an unlikely Florida girl, one with a dream that wouldn't go away.

For four straight seasons, Florida runaway Lisa Andersen dominated the pro women's tour despite (or because of) motherhood and a bad back. Andersen romping in the soup at Off The Wall in 1995

Lisa Andersen

The Inspiration

LISA ANDERSEN, CIRCLING TOWARD HOME

Lisa Andersen was a four-in-a-row women's world surfing champion in the 1990s. For whatever reasons, she was also the catalyst that set off the women's (or girls') surfing renaissance of the 1990s. It was the time, and she was the one. Just the looks, just the style, and everyone said she surfed like a man. There was something fresh and sexy in her, and wounded; everyone carries his or her scars somewhere. But she was successful, and that felt great. She was free, at least freer than she'd ever been, and she was surfing. That was her life—surfing and surfers, and the surfing media. ✺ It is late September of '02, a year after the World Trade Center attacks and a couple of weeks before the Bali bombings, and I am in Seignosse, France. Here and in the adjacent

Lisa Andersen, now looking at the world from both sides, with year-old Erica during the year of her first successful world title campaign, 1994

town of Hossegor, Quiksilver is holding the Roxy Pro France (a $60,000 world championship tour-rated women's competition) and the Quiksilver Pro France (a $300,000 world championship tour-rated men's competition). Andersen has come to surf. I've called her from a phone booth the day before the event (sponsor Siemens, a communications company, has provided competitors and other event VIPs with free cell phones, and the press got free lists of their numbers). She is staying at a house nearby, back in the warren of streets and homes inhabiting the coastal lowland—nice neighborhoods, reasonably wealthy. She said she might be able to meet today, but the waves have come up overnight and now the women's event is on hold until a 1 P.M. decision as to whether or not they will surf today.

The surf along this hundred-mile stretch of white beach is extremely mercurial. It comes and goes with the tides, shifting here, shifting there, as variations in water depth combine with fluctuations in swell to make surfing a moveable feast. That's why these contests are "mobile," with several venue options between here and the Spanish border 100 kilometers to the south. The main stage is in Hossegor, near the Place de Landais, where there are several bars, restaurants, and hotels right at the famous surf spot known as Le Nord. Quiksilver's team manager, a guy named

"She surfs like a man," was the ultimate compliment paid to Andersen as she tore through the competition en route to four straight world titles.

Belly, showed me a picture of himself at Le Nord riding a grinding, gnarly twenty-foot wave. The photo was shot in January, when this corner of the Bay of Biscay becomes a catcher's mitt for mean roundhouse low-pressure systems swinging down from the shoulders of Greenland. You have to really want it to get it then.

But this is September, and a late one at that—very mild, almost sultry, and the waves glassy. It was flat all summer, so there is a little pressure on contest organizers to get started if there are any waves at all. The last men's contest, the Figueira Pro in Portugal, ended in a difference of opinion. On the world championship tour (WCT), contestants have a say in whether they surf or not. In Portugal, the pros opted to wait for better swell, while organizers and sponsors pressed them to surf what waves there were. In the end, the swell died completely, and the event was canceled.

At Seignosse, shortly after 1 P.M., the decision is made to begin the women's event. A weak swell is pulsing in from the west, and the tide has dropped enough to get the waves breaking a little farther out from shore, peaking and peeling off to the right and left as defined by the shape of the buried sandbars. Conditions are good, but there are long stretches between waves.

Andersen stands on the wet sand in her blue singlet. She has left eighteen-month-old Mason up on the beach with Nicole, a friend who's come along with them to Europe; Erica, nine, is home in Florida with Andersen's mother, which strikes me as a little ironic.

I'll explain. In 1983, Andersen came south from the hills of Fork Union, Virginia, to the shores of Ormond Beach, Florida, where she discovered surfing. Accustomed to playing in the creeks and exploring the wonders of the countryside, the fourteen-year-old girl found solace in the warm Atlantic waves. She skateboarded, tried everything, but surfing was the best. When a swell hit, she'd head to the beach, walk maybe five ramps up-current, and throw herself onto her borrowed board to paddle out into incessant sets of relentless whitewater that would sweep her along the beach, past where'd started out, until she'd finally give up, come back to shore, and walk back up the beach to try again. She pined to make it "outside" where young men surfed green, unbroken waves.

Eventually, she made it out there, and the rest is history. Andersen was a quick study. She wanted to get away from her Ormond Beach home, where her Danish father was a drinker who relied on "whippings" for rule enforcement, and her New York–born mother (Andersen was born on Long Island in 1969) was caught in the middle but generally seconded his motions. Andersen loved the freedom and calm out on the ocean, but she loved to compete, too (she was the lone girl on her Little League team back in Fork Union). She freely challenged the other surfers. The boys called her Trouble.

Her parents responded to her surf mania with resistance, demanding her nightly attendance at a 5:30 meal, and no going out afterward. She was the lone female on the Seabreeze High School surfing team, but they wouldn't give her money for entry fees. She persisted and finally got into a couple of contests, coming sixth (out of six) in the first and second (out of two) in the other.

Life was a disaster. What she saw as a healthy, sane activity, her parents viewed as a low-life activity that put her in with the worst sort of people—beach bums and druggies. Her mother forced her to take a drug test; she was concerned that Lisa might be predisposed to go the way of her father. But the girl was aided and abetted by one of the older surfers, a twenty-something guy who dreamt of becoming the best surfboard glasser in the world; he gave her surfboards and rides to the beach. When he moved to California, he wrote her letters encouraging her to follow, and eventually she did. Andersen took off right after school got out in June of '85; she left her mother a note saying she would one day be the world champion of women's surfing, although she wasn't sure there was such a thing.

Andersen bought a one-way plane ticket (her first flight ever) to Huntington Beach, California—Surf City, USA—and hooked up with the guy from Florida who, it turned out, was "weird-strange in a kind of way." They lived in a one-bedroom upstairs apartment in a building a couple of blocks from the pier. She sat out on the roof nights with her headphones on, while punk bands shredded the air downstairs, and rode her skateboard to the beach, where she worked hard to excel. She made a small wage cleaning tables at an Italian restaurant, and for months, her mother never knew where she was.

Potent bottom turn out of the pit of a meaty Kaua'i barrel— Andersen at the peak of her powers, with three titles under her belt and shooting for a fourth, 1996

And then one weekend there was a contest, a National Scholastic Surfing Association (NSSA) event. The girls' competition was on Sunday morning, and she got there early. The site was all set up (they'd run the men's heats the day before), and she found a nice resting spot under a table. When Australian surf icon Ian Cairns found her sleeping there an hour later, she asked him if she could enter the contest. Alas, he said, since you are not in school and hardly a resident, I cannot, as head coach of the NSSA team, admit you. "But please," she said, and he relented. And she knew he knew she'd signed her mom's signature on the entry form.

"I won that contest," she said. "I won pretty much every one. That was cool."

Andersen accumulated quite a collection of trophies, all the same height. She sent the newspaper clippings to her mother. By Thanksgiving weekend, '86, she had a little surf-media buzz going. She made the NSSA team to the United States Amateur Surfing Championships and won it. The event was held in Florida, not far from her home. After some rapprochement, Andersen returned to Huntington Beach, where Craig Comen, team manager for Aleeda Wetsuits, offered her three wetsuits a year in exchange for a sticker on her board. Eventually he invited her into the house he shared with rising pro Greg Mungall and his wife. A good friend of theirs was a highly regarded central California surfer, Dave Parmenter.

After winning a couple of pro-am events and seeing the cash go to lower finishers, Andersen determined to go pro herself and sought out a tour sponsor. She finally caught the attention of Bob Hurley, the savvy head of surfwear company Billabong USA and a familiar face around Huntington. In fact, Hurley had been keeping Andersen in her favorite men's boardshorts for some time, but when she begged a ticket to Japan for the Marui Pro, he was reluctant; surf companies didn't sponsor women. In the end, he told her that, if she didn't find someone else to send her, he would.

Thus it was that Andersen found herself near Chiba's Torami Beach in October of '87, bivouacked in one of the Billabong team houses with a passel of top pros. She noticed that Parmenter was staying in the other Billabong house. Well, she and Dave were soon romantically involved; they were an item for several years, traveling and training together, spending time with Tom and Marie Curren and other notables. Andersen found herself regularly riding waves with some of the best in the world. She surfed almost exclusively with men, and Parmenter was one of the very best coaching talents in the sport.

Although she shared ninth place with the other first-round losers in Japan, Hurley kept Andersen on the Billabong team with a $5,000 contract that covered airline tickets and little else. She ended the tour with a fifth to finish twelfth in the ratings and earn Rookie of the Year honors. The following year, Hurley upped her contract to $8,000, and she did it all over again—more ninths. But life on the tour was mostly misery and poverty—sleeping on floors, schlepping gear, mooching rides, scrounging for food, dodging sexual politics (lesbian surfers were a hot topic at the time).

Andersen won her first ASP pro events in '90. After arriving in Australia with forty dollars in her pocket, she won the Burleigh Heads event and $8,000, then went south to Bells Beach and won there, too—another $5,000. Next, she took third place in Sydney, winning another $2,500 and earning the three-event grand slam title and a bonus $5,000. For the first time in her life, Andersen had money.

Her success caught the attention of American surfwear giant Ocean Pacific (Op), which signed her to a lucrative three-year deal. Op was mounting a major campaign around its two rising stars—Andersen and Kelly Slater—when the company filed bankruptcy. Andersen was back to square one, looking ahead to a new year with no sponsor in sight.

This time she approached Bruce Raymond, a former pro surfer and a key man at Quiksilver. Quik had recruited Slater from Op just before the bankruptcy,

Sweeping top turn at Off The Wall, one of Andersen's favorite North Shore spots, December 1997

Andersen on the beach in Florida, 1997—the year of her fourth consecutive (and final) world title

and Raymond (a former pro surfer himself) was sympathetic to Andersen's situation. He cannibalized tight budgets and got her to Australia, where she again won at Bells Beach, this time with a Quiksilver logo on her board, in the company's hometown (Torquay), with its founders (John Law and Alan Green) looking on. It was beautiful, and she was Quiksilver's girl from then on. As the public face of Roxy, the company's women's line, she proved a powerful role model for a new wave of female surfers inspired by her grit, masterful wave riding, and those neat clothes she wore. Plus, the word was, she surfed like a man.

Ironically, Andersen's four world titles came after she gave birth to her daughter, Erica, in '93. Her relationship with Parmenter had ended, and the father of the baby was an ASP head judge from Brazil. Andersen became the first single mom traveling with a baby on the pro tour, and somehow the situation had a galvanizing effect on her. She won three events in each of the following three tours (1994 through '96), and then won five events in '97 for an unprecedented fourth consecutive world title.

Chronic back problems forced Andersen off the tour midway through the '98 season, and her life drifted back to Florida, where she fell in love with Paul Osbaldiston, a New Zealander with a landscaping business, who is the father of Mason; the four of them (including Erica) live on the river in Ormond Beach. In honor of her achievements, the ASP agreed to give Andersen a comeback shot with a yearlong "wild-card" entry for '02 WCT events.

Which brings us back to the beach in France, '02, where Andersen, standing on the wet sand in her blue singlet, has been joined by Megan Abubo and Keala Kennelly, two of the hottest Hawaiian surfers. Kennelly was a standout presence in the recent Hollywood hit film, *Blue Crush,* which depicts women's surfing as it hardly could have existed had it not been for Lisa Andersen. But this is no movie, this is inconsistent high-tide Hossegor, and the beginning of this first three-woman heat of the day is probably premature. Andersen manages to catch one decent wave, then languishes as time runs out and the ocean fails to deliver. Abubo and Kennelly advance, while Andersen heads for a round-two second-chance heat.

That chance comes as the last heat of the day, held late in the lowering gloom. The ocean was obliging throughout the intervening heats, but now it is book-ending the day with a rising tide and another lackluster lull. The sea appears to have nothing for her, and she doesn't seem surprised. The two other women get their waves, and Andersen is out of the contest.

Two days later, we meet at the house where she's been staying with friends. She is packing up, heading home, leaving in the morning. Nicole takes Mason for a stroll so we can talk.

"I really got those pretty bad heats," she explains. "I don't like that desperate feeling when you're in a heat, five minutes left, and you're desperate. You're desperate, you don't want to lose, don't want to lose . . . and then you're, like, "I'm losin'. The harsh reality here is that there's nothing coming, and it's over. It's a really rotten feeling."

She tells me about her life and her family and the tour. She describes her most recent near-death experience, during the Billabong Pro at Teahupo'o earlier in the year. In her semifinal heat against fellow four-time world champ Layne Beachley, she felt pressured to take a set wave that came walling in toward the draining live-coral reef, but it ledged beneath her, the bottom fell away, and she drove straight into the bottom. She went over the falls twice and was heading for certain trouble when lifeguard Rusty Keaulana roared in on his PWC. It was a complicated rescue, performed under the duress of a pummeling set of waves, but they got her out of a very bad situation. Teahupo'o is reputed to be the world's most dangerous wave; an aspiring Tahitian surfer was killed there in April of 2000, sliced open from chin to chest by the coral.

"It's not a place I think we should be competing," Andersen says. "Only because I have more to lose—family. If something happened to me, I'd be just. . . . What's the point? Why risk your life?"

She talks for quite a while. She's used to telling her story. A film of that story has been in development at Warner Brothers for some time, and she's had to download her life to a succession of scriptwriters, none of whom have quite nailed it. But working on it has given Andersen a wonderful access to her own caravan of memories, many of them difficult, but nonetheless honed into anecdotal jewels. Though soft-spoken and understated, she's world-wise and witty. If she hasn't seen it all, perhaps she's seen enough.

"The tour never really gets anywhere," she says. "It's the same old spots, same old dilemmas, same old things, but then you don't want to go down that path. You really want to see the upside of the thing, but sometimes you get a sense of everything and, 'Whoa! What am I doing here? Should I go back home?' And then when I was pregnant, and I wasn't around any of it, I saw how good the waves were, and I'm, like, 'I have to go for it again.' So I got fired up, and then halfway through the year, you're like, 'What fire? What was I thinkin'?'" And the next day she flies home to Florida.

New technology allows water photographers to capture intimate images of wild and extreme moments, fanning the flames of celebrity even for these athletes who do their thing far from shore. Brad Chisholm in deep, 2000

Life in the real world was growing increasingly unreal in the latter decades of the twentieth century. Webs of civilization—extensions of nineteenth-century Manifest Destiny—were binding the world to a new corporate order, a colossal global infrastructure of capitalistic firmware engineered by lawyers and bankers on behalf of. . . . Well, that was the big question, wasn't it?

As the so-called virtual landscape bifurcated exponentially, the net effect was the shrinking of the boring old three-dimensional Universe. The average Westernized human was, in fact, spending very little time in the natural world. As all forms of media (from television to computers to cell phones) proliferated, the prophetic voices of George Orwell, Aldous Huxley, Marshall McLuhan, and others were systematically silenced precisely as the futures about which they warned were integrated into the emerging paradigm.

Meanwhile, the waves kept coming.

At the grassroots level, where the world was both constricting and mundane, overstimulation of the masses was leading inevitably to desensitization. New generations were forced to seek physical, sensual context through new avenues—often-violent ones. For those blessed with opportunity, "extreme" became the big draw for participant and voyeur alike, as the rank-and-file migrated from team sports to board sports.

The archetype of board sports was surfing, maligned by the mainstream press in the 1950s as the idle activity of beach bums and satirized throughout the ensuing decades as simply vacuous. Prototype for alternative or outlaw sports, surfing spawned skateboarding in at least two creative outbursts—the steel-wheeled '60s and the urethane-wheeled '70s—then calved off the logical seasonal complement, snowboarding. Variations on these pastimes defined some of the richest veins in Western subculture by Y2K.

Surfing, skateboarding, and snowboarding were the hot sports, the hot lifestyles; these activities and their fashion accouterments became ubiquitous. Several small swim-trunk companies, started in unknown beach towns in the '60s and '70s, swelled into diverse multinational corporations by the year 2000. As the primitive local surfing competitions of the '60s transformed into the immense seaside circuses of the '80s and '90s, the top talents found themselves developing some serious street value.

Australian Tom Carroll, Californian Tom Curren, and South African Martin Potter rose to rock-star status in the '80s, dueling from continent to continent for the world title. Here were young, attractive professionals with plenty of grit, style, and charisma. Thousands jammed the beaches to watch them engage with the dangerous near-shore wilderness. Carroll snagged the sport's first million-dollar contract, courtesy of the wildly successful surfwear brand Quiksilver.

By the '90s, the stage was set for the arrival of a gifted athlete who would take surfing to a new level, a surfer who seemed able to go anywhere on a wave that he could imagine. Nothing and nobody could compare with this kid from Florida, a surfer who could tame the wild and bring it right home to your living room.

Kelly Slater

The Teacher

The day after Lisa Andersen leaves France, a new swell lights up La Nord. Officials are calling it five to six feet, but it looks a lot like eight to ten to me, and sometimes ten to twelve. Surfers are concerned with such things; size matters, and the cool thing, since time immemorial, has been to understate it. At a place like Hossegor, a four-foot wave can easily snap your board. ⁂ By most people's standards, this particular Friday morning is more than snappy. As a morning haze dissolves into sunlight, the surface of the ocean—dark blue and green and slick as glass—slowly undulates with approaching bands of swell. Manicured by a light offshore breeze, each wave crests and curls in conformity to the under-lying water depth; on this particular day that means

The generally small, warm waves of Florida have been a training ground for many champion surfers. Floridian Kelly Slater on his way toward winning the 2002 Quiksilver In Memory of Eddie Aikau contest in big waves at Waimea Bay

157

long smooth walls curling into tubular shapes and peeling like zippers both north and south.

The surfing is brilliant, the area directly in front of the main stage of the Quiksilver Pro France packed with scores of competitors racing to ride a few waves before the contest begins. When it does, nine second-round heats are run before contest director Rob Brooks rolls the thing straight into round three, featuring (some would say starring) six-time world champion Kelly Slater (now thirty), who's been off the tour for a few years but is back, courtesy of a yearlong "wild-card position," which the ASP granted him in consideration of his status in the sport. It was this first-ever deal between the ASP and Slater that helped open the door for Andersen's comeback shot. Without such wildcard positions, these surfers would have faced the arduous gauntlet of the ASP's World Qualifying Series, which neither former champion was willing to attempt. So this was a good way to welcome them back.

Taj Burrow is a young Australian who rides for Billabong, Quiksilver's largest rival; he's a great surfer—explosive, gymnastic, and fast. He and Slater wade into the water for their round-three heat as time is running out for Australia's Danny Wills in his contest with South Africa's Paul Canning. As Canning and Wills headed for the beach, Slater moves farther out and into position to pick off a developing peak. It crests just as the air horn sounds, beginning the heat, but Slater hesitates, turns the nose of his board away from shore, and slips out through the fringing lip.

A couple of minutes later, another set arrives; its first wave is bigger and catches both surfers inside. Duck-diving and popping out the back, Burrow finds himself in the perfect place for the second wave as Slater paddles over its shoulder and strokes an arc straight into the lifting hood of the third. The thing walls long and straight in front of him, and Slater drops into the pit, whips his board around into the fastest high-line drive of the day, somehow loses control, and—suspended momentarily upside down, fully extended, as relaxed as a rag doll—takes the wipeout of the event right on the head.

But Burrow's luck runs out, as Slater snags another good wave and stitches it with a series of profoundly understood maneuvers, dealing with the dynamically concaving water surface as if it is a skateboard park with which he is intimately familiar. He goes on to win the heat by a compelling 17.80 to 11.50 margin.

The following dawn smacks of southern California, a slight tang of smog in the air. The swell is smaller but impeccable as the

As America's top amateur surfer, Slater duked it out with his California pal Rob Machado to win the 1989 Op Junior at Huntington Beach, California. The following year, Slater went pro.

A wave is often what a surfer makes of it. Here, Slater's snaking wake reveals the nuances of his slashing trajectory across a performance-friendly Malibu swell.

first heat of round four takes to the water—Canning vs. Slater. Shortly after the horn, a dark band of swell sweeps in and wedges into a clean peak. Slater takes off on the north side of the fringing crest, carves to his right, and ducks under the cover of the folding lip. As the wave unravels, he perfectly matches the speed of his board to the peeling curl. The impression is of a precisely choreographed slow-motion dance between surfer and wave, from which Slater emerges unscathed.

His next wave is as clean and perfectly shaped as the first. Again, he back-doors the section as it folds over and comes skating out the end. Then he pumps his legs to go back high and drives into a second section, which closes with a *whump!* behind him as he charges out the other end and races down the line. Nobody else has really had a tube all day, and Slater gets two on one wave. Typical.

Back on the beach, after a debriefing by the ASP's own interview team, Slater stands at the entrance to the fenced area adjacent to the complex of portable structures housing judges, announcers, media, VIP seating, a large scoreboard, and other event infrastructure. With his wetsuit peeled down low on his hips, he reflexively palms the short stubble on his head as he poses for photos with kids and young surfers and moms and dads. He is patient and polite as he signs posters and T-shirts. He seems to have time for everyone.

This all started about ninety miles up the beach, where, as America's eighteen-year-old "new school" sensation, Slater defeated reigning world champ Martin Potter in the opening round of the '90 Quiksilver Lacanau Pro and was immediately mobbed by hundreds of autograph-seekers. Security guards intervened, while the thrilled young man assured the crowd he'd stay on the beach signing autographs until everyone was satisfied, and he did, and they were.

For the next eight years, on a torrid path to those six world titles, this kid from Florida was the object of thousands of fans at every accessible event on the tour. As amazing as he was in the water (he has been considered the best surfer in the world for over a decade), Slater also exuded a mix of boyish innocence and sexual charisma that proved compelling to groupies and media alike. He was talented, smart, and beautiful, and his timing was perfect.

THE SLATER SAGA IS WELL KNOWN in the surfing world. He was born in Cocoa Beach, Florida, in 1972. His father (Steve), a surfer and former lifeguard, had a bait and tackle shop when the kids were young; Steve's wife (Judy) raised the kids—Sean, Kelly, and Steven. The brothers grew up surfing and fishing, taking every opportunity to escape their small home, where never-ending financial problems were lubricated by alcohol (Steve and Judy divorced when Kelly was eleven). Surfing by age five, Kelly was eight when he entered his first contest at the local beach (Third Street) and won the "menehune" (Hawaiian for "the little people") division, riding his small twin-finned body board.

Cocoa Beach has some of the finest surf in Florida and, over the years, many of America's best surfers learned the sport here. The town's most celebrated spot, Sebastian Inlet, is on the north side of a rock-and-timber jetty that borders the man-made entrance to the Indian River estuary. Incoming swells reflect off the jetty creating a wedgelike effect that can double the size of the waves and make them especially challenging. Naturally, competition is intense, with many skilled surfers vying for relatively scarce waves. It was a perfect training ground for the precocious Slater, who began scratching for a place in the rotation when he was little more than ten years old. That was '82, the year he won the first of a half-dozen East Coast surfing titles.

As one of the kids coached by local legend Dick Catri ("do as I say, not as I do"), Slater soon won the "superheat" at Dave "Surf Nazi" Hart's annual birthday contest up in Jacksonville, earning a first-prize round-trip ticket to Hawaii. On the North Shore, the twelve-year-old kid got his first taste of mid-Pacific power (much

Opposite: Charging out of the pit at G-land during the 1997 Quiksilver Pro, Slater holds a line toward a floating gallery of spectators at this remote world-class surf spot in Java. Although derailed by Australian Luke Egan in this particular event, Slater stayed on track for the year to win his fifth world title.

Evening splendor—like a swooping bird, Slater finds a solo path at Backdoor Pipeline in December of 1993

different from Florida's relatively gentle surf). His surfing steadily matured, and, in '87, he won both the junior and open men's divisions when Australian and U.S. amateurs met at the Pacific Cup in Queensland.

In the summer of '90, Slater entered his first pro contest, the Life's a Beach Classic in Oceanside, California, losing to event winner Martin Potter in the second round. A few weeks later, in the process of winning his first professional event (the Body Glove Surf Bout) and $30,000 in perfect waves at Lower Trestles, he signed a new contract with Quiksilver right there on the beach—just in time for his revenge over Potter at the Quiksilver Lacanau Pro, where he later lost to Tom Curren, who was charging for his third world title.

It was a dizzying pace, and along the way, Kelly attracted unprecedented media attention. He proved to be the rare individual who more than fulfilled the expectations imposed on him. And all the while, he'd relentlessly attended his Florida high school, from which he graduated in June of '91 with a 4.0 average.

Slater seemed to be good at everything. His mother gave him a guitar for graduation, and within a couple of years, he and a posse of surf pals formed a band called Fear of Hair (later The Surfers). His Los Angeles–area agent, Bryan Taylor (who recognized his potential as a fourteen-year-old grommet), parlayed Slater's '92 selection as one of *People*'s "50 Most Beautiful People" into a role on *Baywatch*, the world's most popular television show. That same year Slater won his first ASP world title (the youngest champ ever at twenty), but his focus wandered (or was overwhelmed by that bevy of *Baywatch* babes) in '93, and he dropped to sixth on the tour. Feeling the pressure from pro peers, who saw his role as Jimmy Slade (the

surfer with a yellow Chevy van and a double-agent's life) as a commercial sellout, he left the show and won five consecutive world titles (1994–98). His fame reached a crescendo in the mid '90s (eight-page swimsuit special in *Sports Illustrated*, the cover of *Interview*, modeling for Versace, antidrug ads, etc.), when he entered an on-again, off-again relationship with *Baywatch* sensation Pamela Anderson. Meanwhile, he started playing golf and discovered he was good at that, too.

Slater stepped away from the pro tour in '99. His relationship with Anderson over, he still surfed in and won a few premier events (his fifth Pipeline Masters, the Quiksilver in Memory of Eddie Aikau at Waimea Bay, the Gotcha Pro Tahiti), but mainly he traveled to exotic parts of the world and rode perfect waves for exclusive cameras, and he worked on his golf game, and he fathered a child (Taylor). And how it's 2002 and he's back—a yearlong wildcard on the WCT. It hasn't been a great year, but it's had its moments.

TWO DAYS AFTER THE QUIKSILVER Pro France wraps up, I meet Slater at his home away from home in the hills above Bidart, just down the coast from Biarritz. Situated on the edge of a virtual parkland, the spacious, artfully decorated house is owned by Harry Hodge, cofounder of Quiksilver Europe and chairman/CEO of Quiksilver International, the billion-dollar global "boarding" company. When he's visiting, Slater occupies a modest guest room.

I sit at the snack bar; Slater stands opposite, in the kitchen, keeping the juice and fruit flowing. He lost his semifinal heat to Hawaiian Andy Irons on a questionable wave score in the last two minutes of the heat, but he seems to take it in stride.

The star of late '80s "new school" surfing, by the time he turned pro, Slater had revolutionized the top-end of the sport. This radical roller coaster ride at the Chiemsee Pipe Masters in December 1995 illustrates the wunderkind's imaginative brilliance. Surfing with amazing confidence, Slater won the event, locking up the Hawaiian Triple Crown and his third world title.

"It was awful," he admits, referring to his heat against Irons. "But I very rarely blame judges, I just blame the system. It's difficult, and it's not as fair as it could be." He explains his own ideas for improving the system, eliminating situations whereby one mistake can take a surfer out of an event. "I'm putting in a submission this week," he says. "We're gonna create a leader-board type system, like golf, so if you lose a heat, you don't lose the contest. We all surf an equal number of times throughout the contest, and then you make a cut—that sort of thing."

As it happens, Slater has many ideas, most significantly about America's disconnect with the rest of the world post-September 11, 2001. "I'm sittin' with my girlfriend watchin' the TV, and we're crying, and the first thing that came to my mind was, well, we've done something really bad to somebody. 'Cause nobody's just gonna do this for no reason. We've done something real bad to somebody for a long time, and they're gettin' back at us for it."

Perhaps the ultimate right-hand wave in the world is at Jeffreys Bay on the remote South African coast between Cape Town and Durban. Here, in 1995, Slater handles the freight-train barrel with aplomb.

Opposite top: Slater skimming the cornice at Hollow Trees, setting up his palette for a full-throttle carving cutback, 1999

Opposite bottom: Three-dimensional articulation in the four-dimensional medium of space in time. Slater writes the book.

He expresses concern about President Bush and weapons of mass destruction and the cause of it all. "We as Americans have, let's say, fifty percent of the wealth of the world . . . or more," he says, "yet almost none of us think we have enough. We're underpaid, we're overworked, and I'm not gonna complain about that—I'm overpaid, and I work hard."

He speaks about Noam Chomsky, the renowned and outspoken professor of linguistics, and writer Gore Vidal (he is reading Vidal's 2002 book *Perpetual War for Perpetual Peace*), voting and the electoral college ("If it was a popular vote, I would vote—if we lived in a true democracy"), inventor Nikola Tesla and "free energy," about the efficacy of hydrogen fuel, the big bang ("Was that an orgy?"), pornography ("America's sexually repressed society creates an appetite for the forbidden fruit"), and surfers as environmentalists.

"If you're one, you're the other—you have to be," he asserts. "The reason we're worried about our impact on the world is because we're worried about our lives and our kids' lives, but the earth doesn't need us. If the earth wants to get rid of us, we'll be gone soon. We're nothing to the earth."

We talk about his current affluence: "We grew up with nothin', so I really had to work mentally to be comfortable with being well-off. People think, well, you've got a bunch of money, what are you worried about? But when you have a bunch of money and you think that you're at risk of blowing that money, which was what was happening when I was twenty years old, then it's really kind of frightening to think that you could be set up, and that you could mess that up."

When I ask him about his early influences, he brings up his senior English teacher, "a guy named Mr. Ballantine, who passed away about two years after I got out of school. He was one of those teachers you never forget. He had enthusiasm, and he would give every kid the same amount of attention. There'd be kids who obviously needed more attention, but that wouldn't stop him from giving the smart kids as much attention, too. This guy was equal with everyone; he was an amazing teacher."

Addressing the question of surfing influences, he talks about Tom Curren: "Every turn of Tom's board was like a brushstroke; it meant something. It was leading him to a place he wanted to be on the wave, and it felt like he was just fitting in with the flow of what was happening naturally. It just felt like it went with the natural flow of a wave."

Slater is a student of technique and has been working on a book for surfers. He describes one of his own revelations: "In order to draw that perfect line, your weight has to be balanced in the right places. So, I started grabbing my back right rail to keep my right shoulder down, and when I did, I realized the technique kind of lined up with golf, where you set up for the swing with one shoulder higher than the other. Bringing the back shoulder up and the front one down lowered my center of gravity and put more weight on my back foot while opening the turn up with my shoulders." He's happy about that.

"If you really want to get good, you have to look at your technique. If you look at the pictures of really great turns—Occy [Mark Occiluppo], Curren, Michael Peterson —you'll see the technique in there. You can do something the right way or the wrong way; you either do something the most efficient way or you don't. And if you're not, then how do you fix that?"

He speaks of his dreams of building a revolutionary flex-bottomed surfboard, and then he considers the understandable difficulty of teaching someone to surf: "You're moving with nature, and you have to adjust to what it's doing. You have to figure out how to paddle, how to stand up, how to balance, and you have to do that on something that's moving around . . . and you probably have about one second to do what you're supposed to do, and if you don't, you fall. When you're starting, you could surf for weeks and only gather yourself about two minutes worth of experience."

He comments on his public life: "Sometimes throughout my career I've felt like a zoo animal; I feel kind of caged behind this fence, and everyone's just staring at me to see what I'm gonna eat. It got to a place were I was so famous in this circle that

Despite his great success and enormous worldwide notoriety, Slater remains accessible to fans, fellow competitors, and even the most fledgling of journalists. At Mundaka on the Basque coast of Spain in October of 2002

people thought, 'I have to have an autograph or a picture.' It wasn't really about me, it was about some energy that was happening, some sort of anomaly." He mentions the "vulgar" questions strangers ask him about his relationship with Pamela Anderson. "I can't tell you the number of guys that ask me some sleazy question about Pam, and my response to them is, 'Hey, be a gentleman.'" He considers how his drive to success could be seen as a reaction to his early home life: "Fame and surfing and all the things that have come along with it have been, like, my drug, that would make, like, any pain or issue I have go away."

Slater's mother bought him a guitar for high-school graduation. He developed into an excellent musician, playing on the road with friends Rob Machado, Jack Johnson, Peter King, and others. "A lot of people dream of being musicians," says Slater, "but I've seen a lot of musicians who dream about riding waves. It kind of fits into their free way of thinking."

But now he seems to be looking at the world with a new clarity. "My belief is that heaven and hell are metaphorical terms for what you make of your life. In any instant, you have the ability to make your life total pleasure or total hell, and I know at times my life has been . . . both. Not at the same time, but my life has been what I consider to be hell, when I was totally depressed. . . . When I was a kid, my mom used to say I could jump in a pile of shit and come up smelling like a rose. From a really young age, I've felt like my life was gonna be magical; I knew it was gonna be, and I really didn't have any doubts about it, but I didn't know how it was going to happen. Most anything I've ever set my mind to, I could accomplish. I felt like I was always in the right place at the right time."

I suggest that the evenhanded way he engages the public might reflect the influence of Mr. Ballantine. He considers and says, "You feel power when you go to help someone, when you engage them. It can even be, 'Hey, how'd you end up like this?' or, 'How ya doin' today?' If you engage someone in a way that's not negative, you power yourself up, and you power them up, too." I say he sounds like a teacher.

"I really could argue that I *am* a teacher in some sense," he agrees. "I could argue that I'm teaching . . . I'm helping teach people how to enjoy themselves better. There's a lot of shitty teachers in the world."

After a while, Slater goes into the living room and limbers up on the bare floor. A deftly performed series of yoga contortions—a folding back arch into a dead-solid handstand straight and down into the cobra position—shows surprising strength and flexibility. As he picks up a guitar and begins to play some neat, meditative riffs, I ask what it would be like if all this fame goes away.

"To not have that would probably be somewhat of a shock," he admits. "All of a sudden, I would be faced with myself—with who I am and how to deal with *me*. If I became anonymous today, I'm sure it would happen a lot quicker. We all have some certain bubble that we live in, and to be perfectly honest, mine's a pretty big bubble."

Once upon a time, it was one man, one board, and a limited world of performance. Now it's a quiver of surfboards, each for a specialized range of conditions. With his array of boards, Slater can ride anything from six inches to sixty feet. December 2002 ad shoot for his fin sponsor, FCS

The mother of all great surfing waves—the
spectacular Fijian vortex known as Teahupo'o

Return of the King

The people of Kauai generally held the credit of exceeding all others
in the sports of the Islands. —*Hawaiian Annals* (1822)

Before reaching the inner reefs where surfers ride them, swells approaching Hawaii must first pass over outer reefs—deeper formations, further out to sea. Usually, this passage is uneventful, but when these outer reefs trip giant swells, they set off magnificent avalanches of thunder and mist known as "cloudbreak" surf.

You can watch these waves from the hills above Oahu's North Shore overlooking the spot known as Phantoms or from the cliffs of Maui overlooking Jaws. You can try to judge their size by the time it takes a smoking crest to crack onto the water ahead—*one thousand one, one thousand two, one thousand three, one thousand. . . .* You can imagine riding one, but you know the attempt would be fatal. These are fast waves, moving at nearly open-ocean speed. By the time you could paddle into one, it would be too steep to make it the bottom before it curled over and smashed you to atoms.

Not long ago on Kaua'i, a warrior surfer dreamt of being the first to ride the huge waves at King's Reef, the cloudbreak outside of Hanalei Bay. When his wife gave birth to a daughter, his mother told him to wrap the newborn's *piko* (umbilicus) along with a stone in a ti leaf, then take it to his favorite surf spot. So, he set out to do this. When he arrived at the beach with his surfboard and his small bundle, he was surprised to find the voyaging canoe *Hokule'a* about to set sail for the island of Ni'ihau. Learning of his intent, the ship's pilot welcomed the surfer aboard and gave him the helm. The surfer steered the boat out to the reef, where the *kahuna* (priest) offered a prayer and chanted as the small bundle floated to the bottom. Then the surfer took his board over the side and began paddling back to shore. After a while, he stopped to rest, sat up on his board and looked around. He saw the sun setting and dolphins plunging in the wake of the departing *Hokule'a*. He felt the *mana,* the power, and was grateful.

Titus Kinimaka

The Warrior

TITUS KINIMAKA AND THE SOUL OF HANALEI

Hanalei Bay, a two-mile scoop out of the north shore of Kaua'i, opens onto some twenty million square miles of deep ocean. Out there, far beyond the arc of horizon, pinwheeling low-pressure systems herd vast seas into great swells, which storm these shores each winter. In the shelter of the big bay, in its eastern corner where the green Hanalei River meanders into blue saltwater, a cluster of men, their families scattered happily throughout the tropical parkland around them, stand on the grass above the hard-sand beach where their cars are parked. As they talk and joke, occasionally glancing out at the bay, one of the men seems especially contained and focused.

Arms folded across his chest, Titus Kinimaka studies the waves curling around the distant reef. His eyes are dark and clear, fierce and gentle. His long, dark hair is tied neatly back; sunglasses pushed up on top of his head. The chiseled body, brown and muscled, belongs to a warrior; his face is like the fast-moving clouds overhead, smiling easily at a friend's comment, then gathering back into concentration. For a long time, his eyes remain fixed on the water, even when he speaks, then, finally, he breathes in a long draught of the sweet air and looks around at the dark spires of the perpetually shrouded mountains that buttress this once remote corner of Hawaii's oldest and northernmost island. It is January of 2001, and in one of the last acts of the Clinton administration, the Hanalei has just been protected as one of America's pristine rivers.

KINIMAKA SITS ON ONE OF THE PICNIC TABLES arrayed beneath the palms, strumming a beautiful koa-wood guitar and singing "Dancing in the Sand" in a sweet, soulful voice. Around him sit a cast of regulars, surfers and nonsurfers of various ages. His wife Robin listens dreamily as their daughters Maluhia (Peace) and Mainei Aloha (Gentle Breeze of Love) play over on the grass with the other kids. His younger brother Alikai deftly weaves a basket from a single green palm frond. With most of the long beach occupied by tourists and the well-heeled residents of this newly upscale vacation paradise, I have the feeling that the soul of Hanalei has been painted into this small corner of the bay.

Kinimaka has been coming here to Hanalei since he can remember. The thirteenth of sixteen (eight boys, eight girls) pure-Hawaiian children, he was born in Lihue in 1955. His father was from the Big Island and was well schooled in the old ways. Both he and his wife Ellen were surfers, and most of their children were born on Oahu, where they lived near Waikiki among an extended family of beach-boys and kama'aina, including the immortal Duke Kahanamoku. Kahanamoku took Titus's older brother Percy (Leleo) under his wing, teaching him to dive and paddle and all the other beachboy skills. Percy became a prodigious waterman, and after the family moved to Kaua'i in the early '50s, he started a beach service at the Kaua'i Surf Hotel on Kalapaki Bay near Lihue. Shielded from the open ocean by Kukii Point, Kalapaki's rolling surf was similar to Waikiki's. When Kahanamoku would come over to visit Percy, it was Titus's job to rub oil on his back and make sure he always had two clean towels and a cold drink.

"I was only about six years old," Kinimaka recalls, "but I could feel that this guy's presence had a lot of *mana*. The way everybody was so reverent and respectful, you knew this guy was somebody extraordinary. I remember that he was very mellow, a quiet and gentle person."

Kinimaka's mother taught him to surf when he was three, but it was Percy who schooled Titus in sailing, diving, canoeing, surfboard repair, and countless

Kinimaka ducking under the hood at a secret spot near his Kaua'i home, mid-1980s. Born and raised amid a surfing family with a beachboy tradition, nothing is more natural to him than moments like these.

other skills. Most important of these was water safety and CPR, which translated into a twenty-five-year career as a County of Kauai lifeguard (he met Robin while on duty at Ke'e Beach, out near the end of the road toward Kalalau).

His family's Anahola home was alive with traditional Hawaiian music, and Kinimaka was gifted with a beautiful voice and a talent for the guitar. By age fifteen, he and a partner were earning money playing happy hour at the hotel. Meanwhile, his high school education (he graduated in '73) paled in comparison to the real-world lessons he got from the ocean and from the stories of "uncles" like Waikiki beachboy Rabbit Kekai and Makaha legend Buffalo Keaulana.

Back in the 1960s, the journey north to Hanalei was considerably more difficult. "It was one dirt road all the way down here," Kinimaka remembers. "If you ran into some rain during the day, you couldn't make it out, so you had to be prepared to stay for a couple days. But it was beautiful back then and getting trapped down here when it rained—not too bad! I remember surfing out here when there was nobody around. I'd be getting tube ride after tube ride and there'd be, like, *nobody* to see it. And we used to think, 'Oh God, I wish somebody'd seen that tube ride!' I guess I wished too hard."

There are few better training grounds for surfing than Hanalei Bay. A long, playful wave when it's small, Hanalei reveals quite a different face when those big north swells arrive. "When it's over fifteen feet, Hanalei turns into a kind of monster," Kinimaka explains. "You can't really see this monster coming, but you can feel it. They say the sets come from 'underneath'—you paddle over a wave, and there it is. The bottom drops out, and it's a tube ride all the way."

As a young man honing his skills here and at Kaua'i's other challenging spots, Kinimaka was surrounded by great mentors—Carlos Andrade, Joey Young, Eddie Panui, Jimmy Lucas, Joey Cabell—and soon earned a reputation as one of the island's most dominating surfers. "They all inspired me to charge," he says. "It was all about charging, and it was about soul, and everything you did was from the heart, from the pure love of the sport."

He was quick to embrace the short boards in the winter of 1967–68. "It was fresh," he says of the revolution. "It revived all my senses. The shortboards reflected the freedom of the time." But that freedom translated into a sudden influx of surfers and hippies drawn to the warm paradise of Hawaii, and locals soon found themselves competing for space with newly arrived *haoles*, many of whom displayed little respect for the culture they were invading. What resulted was an era of intimidation and occasional violence as so-called "Primo warriors" (Primo being the island's number-one brew at the time) attempted to stem the tide. Back in those days, Kinimaka was one of the most feared of the Kaua'i locals.

"Titus was the guy who said get all the *haoles* out, and I was the enforcer,"

Kinimaka races a folding cylinder as it peels along the perfectly shaped reef at Honolua Bay on Maui, a long right-hand point wave that is similar in quality to Kinimaka's home break at Hanalei Bay on Kaua'i, mid-1980s

Kinimaka skimming along on the nose, enjoying playtime on a small day at Poipu Beach on Kaua'i—puffy clouds in a blue sky, warm air and water . . . just another day close to his roots in paradise, July 1999

says Alikai, holding up the finished basket. "He did what he had to do, and I did what I had to do." He flashes a big, warm smile.

"I look back on it as the darker times of surfing," Titus admits. "The idea was that all the waves were our inherited right, and we didn't have to share them. . . . I had mixed feelings about it, even then. I realize now that *Aloha* is the way to go, but at the time I was too blind and too young to understand."

Word of the hostility toward *haole* surfers (and photographers who advertised the island's waves) had an enduring impact; even now, you aren't likely to see a camera at any of Kaua'i's best surf spots. It also has effectively kept the crowds down so that today's kids ("our future," Kinimaka calls them) can still experience the same joys of surfing that he had.

Sacrifices have been involved, however. Because surfing contests are famous for attracting attention to remote areas, keeping Kaua'i's beaches local and low-key kept such events out of the picture, which meant that if Kinimaka wanted to be a professional surfer, he'd have to do it against the odds . . . and he did. Minus the usual competitive resume, the Kinimaka reputation was sufficient to earn him invitations to the last two Duke Kahanamoku contests at Sunset Beach ('79 and '80), where his performance was sufficiently outstanding to warrant invitations to all of the prestigious Eddie Aikau memorial events held annually (as long as the surf is over twenty feet and deemed rideable) at Waimea Bay since '86.

Winning "The Eddie" (as the Quiksilver in Memory of Eddie Aikau contest is commonly known) became a mission for Kinimaka. "I lived for that contest," he recalls. "I changed my whole life for it. I quit drinking, quit partying, trained every day, changed my diet. I was up everyday at 4 A.M. to do two hours of floor exercises, an hour of yoga and meditation, then run and swim, then surf all day." He trained for months; his whole life was focused on the most prestigious big-wave surfing event in the world.

Kinimaka spent the night before Christmas, 1989, at the home of water-photographer Don King, right on the beach, less than half a mile from Waimea. The shorebreak there pounds hard, and when the waves get over ten feet, the house's doors start to rattle from the shock waves in the air. If the waves got big enough for the contest, he would be ready; in the meantime, he would surf the bay whenever it broke.

"I woke up at 3 A.M., and the ocean was bombing," Kinimaka recounts. "It was like there was a war going on. I was so excited, I couldn't sleep, so I got up and did my stretches and worked out until the sun started coming up, then I paddled out. I wanted to be the first one there, but a girl was already outside on a boogie board. The waves were a perfect fifteen to eighteen feet, and I had a great time all morning. I decided to catch one last wave and was sitting at the peak when the other surfers started paddling outside for a set."

Kinimaka stayed put, figuring he'd be sure to catch the first wave of the set. But when the wave stood up, it was steeper than he expected. He spun his board toward the beach and dropped almost vertically down the face. Without purchase, he couldn't begin his turn until he reached the bottom of the wave, and by then the section ahead of him was curling over at the top. Thinking it would be hollow enough to fit through, he aimed high and backdoored the section.

"I thought it was gonna stay open, but it collapsed on top of me. I tried to power through, but the board compressed down and spun out sideways and chopped into my right leg. Then the wave's tumbling me around, and when I finally got to the surface, here came another one, so I dove under and got tumbled around again, and when I finally came up there was something hitting me on the side of my cheek, back by my right ear. I was kind of dazed, wondering, 'What *is* this thing?' and I grabbed it and was looking at it, and then I realized it was the bottom of my foot. I couldn't believe it was my foot—that it belonged to me—and I started calling for help, and my friend Louie Ferreira paddled over and took one look and goes, 'Aw, Titus! Broken femur, brah. Broken femur!' And I was so obsessed with the Eddie Aikau thing—training so hard, just out of control—that all I could say to Louie was, 'Oh shit, brah! You think I'm gonna make the contest or what?' What was I thinkin'? I was possessed."

Kinimaka at Hanalei with his tow-surfing equipment, January 2001. The personal watercraft (also known as a jet ski) is essential for getting into giant surf, where human paddling strength won't get the job done.

It was like slamming on the brakes hard, and Kinimaka went into a skid. He was lying on his back in a hospital with a head full of broken dreams. "I couldn't believe it was over," he remembers. "I was lying in the hospital with a broken femur feeling sorry for myself; I was blown away. And then something came to me and said, there are two ways you can do this: be a couch potato, crying and whining about it, or you can get out of bed, get on the floor, and start doing some pushups, so that's what I did."

To minimize his downtime, Kinimaka had opted for the surgical implantation of an eighteen-inch-long steel rod, which was inserted through his right hip and down into the femur to stabilize the bone for faster healing. It was extremely painful, but the surgeon said that if he was careful and lucky, he might be walking again in six months. Meanwhile, if the large incision in his hip became infected, there would be serious consequences.

"The doctor told me six months," says Kinimaka, "but he didn't know me. I used will and prayer to speed up the healing process. I would go into a meditative state, visualizing the bone healing, and I focused my will that there wouldn't be any kind of infection in the incision, and that it would heal from the inside out. Right after I woke up in the morning, I would go into this state. I would focus on the pain, and the pain would take me into an out-of-body state. I would go through all this light, with all these different colors shooting by, and I ended up on the other side of the light. I was in this garden-like place, and I came up to this plantation-style house, and there was a big fish pond full of lilies, frogs, and swans. There was a beautiful willow tree hanging down in front of the house, and I'd walk up onto the deck—a big, wide deck with an oiled floor—and there was beveled glass on the doors and windows . . . it was just a beautiful place to be, and the whole time I was there, I felt no pain in my body. At the same time, if I looked back over my shoulder, I could see myself lying in the bed in the hospital. But if I turned and looked back at the house and garden, I felt no pain in my body. Every day I would do this for about an hour and a half. I understood that I had tapped into some sort of ancient mind-traveling thing. I realized that this must be some kind of energy that every one of us has; we just have to tap into it when we need it. But every time I wanted to go to this place, every day, the only way I could get there was to rub my leg and feel the pain, and then I would go into this state—a deep place, through the light—and I was there again. And after I had stayed there for a while, I'd come back, and I'd feel good. I didn't have any pain in my body."

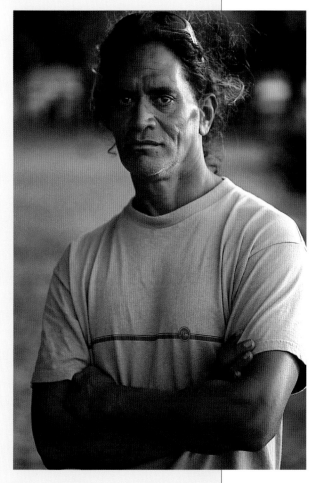

After two months, the doctor ordered an X ray to check on Kinimaka's progress. "He couldn't believe how my scar had healed up so quick, and when he showed me the X ray, there was this ring of calcium that had built up around where my femur had broken, and he asked me, 'What have you been doing?' and I said, 'I've been trying to heal myself,' and he said, 'Whatever you're doing, keep doing it.'

"I kept doing it, but the more it healed, the harder it was to get where I wanted to go. I didn't have the pain to take me there." Four months after the injury, Kinimaka hobbled down the beach at Hanalei and paddled out into ten-foot waves.

"I could stand up and ride," he exclaims. "That meant everything to me because I'd been out of the water for four months—the longest I've ever been out of the water in my forty-two years of surfing." That fall, when the first good north swell hit Hawaii, he was back in the lineup at Waimea. "You gotta get back on the horse and keep going," he laughs. "Otherwise you get gun-shy!"

Kinimaka recovered fully, and his life took some amazing turns. He met his wife, then they had their two daughters. A long-standing sponsorship deal with Quiksilver matured into a magic lifestyle with the creation of the company's Silver Edition line and the selection of Kinimaka to join watermen Melvin Pu'u and David Kalama on a rescue team that would be present at all major Quiksilver events in Europe. He became a vocal advocate for the restoration of Hawaii sovereignty and a defender of the Hanalei River. As his band, Titus Kinimaka and the Kauai Boys, continues to record and perform for a growing audience, his personal training remains intense, guided now by the principles of the "peaceful warrior."

LATE IN THE AFTERNOON, a car comes up the beach and parks nearby. It is Dick Brewer with a new balsa-wood surfboard he's shaped for Kinimaka, who, upon receiving the board, runs his hands admiringly over the smooth contours of its foiled hull. It is an unusual board—short and narrow with hard-chined edges in the rear designed to bite into the faces of the huge waves it has been shaped to ride. Kinimaka's eyes sparkle with anticipation.

For the past five seasons, Kinimaka has been ratcheting up his commitment to tow surfing, riding the giant outer-reef waves with his local partner, Terry Chun. A couple years ago, Kinimaka became the first surfer to ride King's Reef. The swell was so huge, they had to launch at Kinimaka's Hā'ena lagoon and follow rampaging rip currents out between smoking cloudbreaks. When they finally made it to King's the sets were pushing fifty feet, and it was hard to predict exactly where the waves would break. A scary situation took a turn for the worse when Kinimaka was caught inside on a mistimed take-off. Pounded and rag-dolled by a couple of monumental waves, he was held down so long he knew he wasn't going to make it. He was talking to God and had surrendered when it suddenly occurred to him that he was floating over the very spot where he'd left his daughter's *piko* a month before. The moment he realized he wouldn't die alone, he was released. He shot toward the surface and blasted out of the wave. Picked up by Chun, the two proceeded to complete their aim, each surfing one of those magnificent waves, the first ever ridden at King's.

"This is bringing the wood back into surfing," he explains to Brewer, hefting his new towboard. "The tree is a living thing, and this surfboard is still alive—just in a different form. Now, it'll be riding these giant waves that come from halfway across the hemisphere, and it's a pretty heavy combination of energy. Waves are a pure form of energy, you're a pure form of energy [referring to Brewer], and this piece of wood is a pure form of energy. . . ."

"And you're a pure form of energy," Brewer points out.

Kinimaka nods. "All these pure forms of energy . . . there's something going on here." Alert and tuned to the messages of nature, his greatest ambition is to catch a few more giant waves, with his family and his ancestors riding in his heart.

Loose in the juice—a younger Kinimaka shreds the lip of a solid westside Kaua'i wave, December 1979

Beauty's Edge

The beach is a tidal zone, a ragged and chaotic borderland where the interplay of planetary and cosmic forces is perhaps most clearly revealed. As an expression of those dynamics, the surf is beauty's edge, an eternal dialogue between utterly different yet complementary worlds. ⚜ Out on the ragged edges of islands and continents, where whump of wave and surge of sea wears monuments into sand, someone is always watching. They're out there now, following twisted, sodden trails down to the shore. They're leaping from slick boulders into icy brine . . . clawing over thundering cornices into the torquing pits of powerful pulses . . . gliding like gulls across the smooth, glassy slopes of silently advancing swells. Those surfers, those riders of waves. ⚜ Survival out here is always a question of balance. The principle is expressed in the equation "Nature = God" carved into the sandstone above Malibu by Tom Blake. He enlivened the essential surfer's philosophy of respect—for others, for history, for the power of nature. He understood that it was *all* nature. He believed that it was *all* God. The intrinsic sustaining balance of the natural world is self-evident. It is something that is educated into each surfer. If you ride waves long enough and keep your eyes and heart open, you get it. ⚜ There's a million surfers you'll never know or even hear about, pockets of them everywhere, sub-sub cultures where daily "heroics" and communication with the wild plumbs the depths of natural relationships and begs the question of humankind's purpose on the planet. Out of many paths, one path: the way of the surfer.

Index

Index

Acknowledgments

Thanks to all the surfers, photographers, and surf magazine editors and publishers who made this book possible. Big thanks, too, to my editor on this project, Richard Olsen, who offered great support and encouragement.

Parts of this book have appeared in *The Surfer's Path, The Surfer's Journal, LongBoard Magazine, Adrenalin,* and other periodicals devoted to the surfing life and culture.

The *Tao Te Ching* translations are the work of Stan Rosenthal.

Support your favorite beach by joining forces with these and other like-minded organizations:

SURFERS AGAINST SEWAGE
Wheal Kitty Workshops, St Agnes,
Cornwall, UK TR5 0RD
44 (0) 1872 553 001
info@sas.org.uk

SURFRIDER FOUNDATION EUROPE
Pierre Nouqueret, 120 Ave. de Verdun
64200 Biarritz, France
33-5-59-23-54-99
surfrider@wanadoo.fr

SURFRIDER FOUNDATION USA
122 S. El Camino Real, Box 67
San Clemente, CA 92672
(949) 492-8170
info@surfrider.org

Life is a wave, and your attitude is your surfboard. Aim for the light! —Drew

Photo Credits

Erik Aeder: 22, 36, 184–185; Bernie Baker: 122–123; Don Balch: 2–3, 114–115, 117 (right), 182–183, back endpage; Art Brewer: 6–7, 45, 48, 73, 80, 82 (top), 82 (bottom), 84, 85 (left), 85 (right), 88, 119 (right), 120, 132–133, 144, 152, 164 (top), 164 (bottom); David L. Brown Productions: 20; John C. Callahan: 126–127, 132 (left), 137, 158, 161, 165; David Darling: 46, 51, 53, 86; Glen Dubock: spine; Tom Dugan: 76, 151; Jacky "Woody" Ekstrom Collection: 24; John Elwell Collection: 30, 32–33; Alby Falzon: 104; Craig Fineman: 116–117, 130, 174–175, 177 (top), 177 (bottom); LeRoy Grannis: 34–35, 50, 52, 66–67, 67 (right), 68–69, 70–71, 78, 93, 94, 100, 101, 138–139; Walter Hoffman Collection: 23, 25, 26–27; Courtesy Mike Jipp/Lincoln City Surf Shop: 18–19; Joli: 146–147; Thor Jonsson: 8, 10–11, 12–13, 14–15, 186, 188–189; Alex Kampion: 166; Drew Kampion: 4–5, 28 (left), 28 (right), 29, 54–55, 56, 57, 58, 72 (top), 72 (bottom), 81, 90, 91, 96, 98, 99, 102, 103, 106, 107, 118–119, 167, 180, 181; Lee Pegus: 156, 162–163; David Pu'u: 108, 124, 154; Joel de Rosnay: 62–63, 66 (left); Jim Russi: front endpage, 60–61, 64, 74–75, 87, 110, 113, 116 (left), 121, 128, 131, 148, 150, 153, 159, 160–161, 168–169, 170, 172, 178–179; John Severson Collection: 1, 38, 39, 40, 41, 42, 43, 44; Tom Servais: cover, 136, 140, 142–143, 149; Peter Simons: 133 (right), 135 (top), 135 (bottom); United States Postal Service: 16

192